ZE

THORSONS
PRINCIPLES
OF

ZEN

MARTINE BATCHELOR

Thorsons
An Imprint of HarperCollins*Publishers*

THIS BOOK IS DEDICATED TO THE LATE MASTER KUSAN
AND ALL THE PEOPLE IN KOREA WHO HAVE BEEN A
GREAT HELP AND INSPIRATION ON THIS ZEN JOURNEY.

Thorsons
An Imprint of HarperCollins*Publishers*
77–85 Fulham Palace Road,
Hammersmith, London W6 8JB

Published by Thorsons 1999
1 3 5 7 9 10 8 6 4 2

Illustrations in Chapter 5 drawn by Miriam Ellingson
Oxherding pictures by Sokchong Sunim

Martine Batchelor asserts the moral right to
be identified as the author of this work

A catalogue record for this book
is available from the British Library

ISBN 0 7225 3672 0

Printed and bound in Great Britain by
Caledonian International Book Manufacturing Ltd, Glasgow

CONTENTS

INTRODUCTION

Zen has been associated with many different things: Japan, archery, motorcycle maintenance, a certain aesthetic of black and white and pure lines, to name a few. In the past two decades, it has become popular in the West especially in America. Zen has inspired individuals to simplify their lives or to look at them more creatively. Zen has influenced many artists, writers and poets. It has been used in business practices and even in sport to help competitors hone their minds.

Zen actually means meditation. It comes from the word *Dhyana* (Sanskrit). *Dhyana* means meditative state in the Buddhist tradition. This word was transliterated as *Chan* by the Chinese when Buddhism went from India to China. This Chinese character is pronounced *Son* in Korea and *Zen* in Japan.

Zen has many aspects. It has grown within the Buddhist tradition over many centuries in different countries. It has influenced the cultures in which it has developed as well as being deeply influenced and changed by those same cultures. For this reason there are various manifestations of Zen. A Chinese Zen monk or nun does not wear the same robes as a Korean or Japanese one. The temples also look quite different. Chan Chinese temples are very often made of stone and subdued from the outside, Korean Son temples are made of wood and extremely

colourful and Zen Japanese temples are also made of wood but very monochrome.

Zen practice is slightly different from country to country. However, there is a certain body of texts and principles that are common to all Zen schools: the idea of the Mahayana and the Bodhisattva vows; of Buddha nature and of sudden awakening; all of which I shall explain in detail. Zen is about self-development, about experiential practice which helps you to see life directly and to act with wisdom and compassion. It is something that you do while learning not-doing.

I started to practise Zen when I became a Buddhist nun in South Korea. I studied under various Korean Zen masters, in particular Master Kusan, who inspired me with his great kindness, lightness and incisive mind. I stayed ten years and it was an opportunity to practise meditation ten hours a day for six months of the year and to live a Zen monastic life in a traditional Buddhist country. The monastery was nestled deep in the mountains covered with pines, azaleas and maples.

It was a simple life with few amenities and a hot bath once every fifteen days. The days followed the sounds of the bells; it was a disciplined life but also a liberating one. Slowly one realized who one truly was and how one was so deeply connected to the whole world. Zen can be very dramatic but also very ordinary. When I left the monastery and joined a Buddhist community as a layperson in England, my second training started: to put into daily practice what I had learned all these years. Zen has to be lived to be true Zen.

In this book I intend to look at Zen in its manifold aspects so that the reader might have a comprehensive view of Zen and its riches and might be inspired to live a Zen life of love, creativity and freedom.

BASIC IDEAS AND PRINCIPLES

MAHAYANA: THE GREAT VEHICLE

All Zen schools belong to the Mahayana tradition of Buddhism. Mahayana means 'Great Vehicle'. This Buddhist tradition is known as 'Great' because it contains various different approaches to the spiritual path. The different approaches appeal to different people, thereby allowing as many as possible to be liberated from suffering. Zen is not only for monks and nuns but also for laypeople, ordinary men and women. Anyone can practise this path and be liberated regardless of status, knowledge or gender.

A GREAT VOW

One of the characteristics of Mahayana Buddhism is the Bodhisattva ideal. A Bodhisattva is someone who dedicates his or her life to enlightenment and to helping others achieve it for themselves. Bodhisattva means 'Enlightenment Being'. The Bodhisattva practises the six paramitas of generosity, ethics, patience, effort, meditation and wisdom. Paramita (that which has reached the other shore) is generally translated as 'perfection'. By developing and cultivating the six paramitas one is able to reach the other shore of enlightenment.

The Bodhisattva starts on his or her journey by awakening the deep motivation to free all sentient beings from suffering and by taking the Bodhisattva vow, making the firm resolution to attain enlightenment for the sake of all beings. In the Zen tradition, the vow is expressed in a fourfold way. In many Zen ceremonies, the four 'Great Vows' are generally chanted to conclude them. They are also chanted at the beginning of Zen retreats. They are considered the foundation of Zen practice and are the motivation for practice itself.

Sentient beings are numberless, I vow to save them all.
Delusions are inexhaustible, I vow to cut them all.
Dharma gates are limitless, I vow to penetrate them all.
The Buddha's way is unsurpassable, I vow to achieve it.

For a Bodhisattva, the practice is undertaken out of compassion and a great aspiration. One of the important figures in the Zen canon is the Bodhisattva of Compassion (C: Kuanyin, K: Kwanseum, J: Kannon or Kanzeon).* Kuanyin means the all-seeing, all-hearing; the being who hears and sees all the cries and pains of the world. She is represented either as a female figure seated with a slender vase containing a bamboo branch and with a young attendant close by, or standing with a thousand hands and in each hand an eye to see the sufferings of all beings.

There are various practices associated with the Bodhisattva of Compassion. Some people chant the name of Kuanyin over a period of time to help them develop concentration. Some recite various texts or repeat mantras associated with Kuanyin with the aim of focusing on her compassion and mercy. Others invoke the name of the Bodhisattva in times of great difficulties in the hope that Kuanyin might help them due to her great vow to save all beings.

In Zen, compassion is linked with wisdom; the two are inseparable. So it is a compassion that comes from a selfless intention but also a wise intention. We are not being kind because we are expecting something for ourselves or because we know what is best for us is best for other people. We act compassionately after listening to the needs of others and also knowing our own limitations.

Generosity is very much a part of this compassion: being generous in mind and heart towards ourself and others, not being kind only to people we like or who are pleasant to us, nor only when we have plenty of time and it suits us. This Zen compassion could be seen as very altruistic and demanding but as one cultivates Zen one realizes it is within us already, and Zen practice helps us to lower the screens and barriers which stop our natural, wise and equanimous compassion from flowing freely.

BUDDHA-NATURE

In Buddhism, there are various schools of thought about Buddha-nature. Some traditions see it as a seed to develop in practice over aeons and some see it as a natural state that is covered by our delusions and can be uncovered at any time. Zen belongs to the latter approach. The Zen tradition was very much influenced by the Avatamsaka sutra which states that all sentient beings are Buddhas and all Buddhas are sentient beings.

BUDDHA IS MIND, MIND IS BUDDHA

Zen reacted against the idea that enlightenment and Buddhahood were remote conditions; so far away that one might not even get started, being too discouraged by the lengthy process. Zen is saying, 'Look, here and now! We are alive, we can see, hear, taste, smell, think. We can be a Buddha if we only let ourselves be one.' In peaceful and clear moments, but also when we respond wisely and compassionately in difficult circumstances, we realize that they might be more to us than we think. Zen is not about becoming an idealized perfect person but more about living who we are and can be in our more spacious moments.

From this idea of Buddha-nature being intrinsic came the dilemma: why can't we see it and why should we practise? From these questions arose the debate about sudden and gradual awakening and practice which exists to this day in the Zen tradition. Some Zen schools believe that practice and enlightenment are both sudden, which raises the question: Why does it take even ancient Zen masters at least eight to twelve years for any breakthrough to happen and why do they continue to practise afterwards? Korean Master Chinul's way of looking at this debate seems to resolve those questions. He suggests that enlightenment is sudden, followed by gradual practice which in turn might help to provoke more awakenings followed by more practice.

In this scheme, true practice starts after an initial insight which makes us see our true Buddha-nature for a moment, however fleeting. This in turn gives us great confidence in ourselves and the practice. However, there are still many screens and walls of attachment and certain delusions which have to be slowly dissolved through gradual and regular practice. And it is this very dissolution which will help awakenings to occur.

However, one cannot control awakenings. Nothing is guaranteed. It is very easy to say 'let go!', it is very difficult to do it. In the Zen tradition, awakening is often mentioned, but over and over again, Zen masters will advise us not to be caught by the idea and glamour of it. They often say it is like seeing something for the first time that has been with us all along. It is like a fish looking for water until it realizes it is swimming in it, or someone looking for one's head until he or she bangs it on a post and realizes it has been there all the time. So this Zen awakening is not metaphysical and will not take us to some other dimension, nor is it going to transform us in a split second into

Mother Teresa or some venerable ancient Chinese master. But hopefully it will make us more aware of our own innate wisdom and compassion and help us to live more fully from these two qualities. In Zen, it is said:

Buddha is Mind, Mind is Buddha.

THREE TRAININGS: ETHICS, MEDITATION AND WISDOM

Master Kusan used to tell us in his Zen talks that it was essential for all of us as Zen students to train in ethics, meditation and wisdom. These were the basis for any Zen practice. Most importantly they had to be practised in unison. It was like a tripod: with one or two of its legs missing, it could not hold anything and was pretty useless. In the same way, one had to practise the three trainings together for them to be even more effective. A focus on ethics by itself could make one narrow-minded, meditation by itself could make one a little detached and self-absorbed, wisdom by itself could make one a little dry and analytical.

COMPASSION FOR OURSELVES AND OTHERS

Ethics, or morality, are considered important because it has to do with our relationship to the world, people, things and how what we do affects ourselves and others. Zen ethics come out of Buddhist ethics which are based not on rules but on compassion and wisdom, and the notion that as practitioners we intend to dissolve suffering for ourselves and others. In a general way, it answers this question: What would be the most compassionate and wise thing to do? The five basic precepts express this ethic in terms of restraint, of not causing any suffering or more suffering:

do not kill

do not steal

do not have damaging sexual interaction

do not lie

do not take intoxicants.

In terms of positive action, the five precepts are encouraging us to be harmless, generous, disciplined, honest and clear-minded.

These precepts are intended to be cultivated not only in body but also in mind and speech, not only towards others but towards ourselves. Chinul said we had to learn to open and close the precepts, that is to know when to apply them and when, in certain circumstances, not to apply them. The well-known example is: if we were standing in a forest and a deer appeared and ran left, then a hunter appeared, if asked we could reply that the deer turned right.

In the Zen tradition, there are also the Bodhisattva precepts which, in Korea for example, laypeople would retake yearly as a reminder and in the knowledge that one is fallible. These precepts are contained in the Brahmajala Sutra. This is a list of ten major and forty-eight minor precepts. Their intention is to remind us to live with awareness and compassion.

QUIETNESS AND CLARITY

The second training is meditation. When we meditate, we cultivate concentration and enquiry. Concentration helps to still the mind and enquiry helps to make the mind clearer. In order to still the mind, one concentrates on one object. It can be the words of a question (huatou), the breath, the present moment itself. The aim of the concentration is to stay as long as we can with the meditation object. It is quite difficult as the mind has the tendency to wander to the past, to the future, to the shopping list for dinner tomorrow. We need to remind ourselves of our intention to meditate, to focus on the question or the breath, so we have to come back repeatedly to the object of concentration. After a while we come back more quickly and stay longer on the object. Master Hsuyun said:

> A thousand thoughts give us the opportunity to come back to the question a thousand times.

So being distracted is not the problem, *staying* distracted is!

The effect of concentrating and coming back is threefold. First, our mind is more peaceful because there are fewer thoughts engaging it, since we are concentrating on one thing. Secondly, our thoughts become less agitated and obsessive because we do not feed and indulge in our patterns and habits of mind like ruminating, judging, daydreaming, planning, fabricating, etc, as we come back again and again and cut their threads. Thirdly, we are more aware of ourselves and our surroundings as each time we come back, not only do we come back to the question or the breath but we also come back to the present moment. This has the effect of allowing us to be truly aware, alive and present, experiencing this life, this being.

The other aspect of Zen meditation is cultivating enquiry and brightness of mind. This is done by questioning, looking deeply, staying alert in awareness. It stops the mind becoming dull. The aim of meditation is to cultivate a state of mind which is equally quiet and bright. Meditation is not only about relaxing the mind but also about the mind being clear and sharp and through that the mind can be used to its fullest potential for understanding and wisdom. Slowly, one learns to see the world in a different way, more open and full of potential.

POTENTIAL FOR CHANGE

The third training is wisdom. Zen wisdom, in simple terms, is knowing to drink out of a cup, that it is a cup and not a bucket, and being fully present in the drinking, the taste of the tea, its colour, its fragrance, with no grasping of the cup, the tea or ourselves or anything else apart from that. It is not about how many books we have read or how much intellectual knowledge we have accumulated. It is about seeing the characteristics of life which in Buddhist terms are impermanence, unsatisfactoriness and emptiness or non-self.

In Zen, impermanence and death are often impressed upon one. But this does not make Zen people gloomy or pessimistic – on the contrary. By experiencing or understanding impermanence deeply we realize the preciousness of life and the potential for change. It is very easy for us to take life and people for granted. We generally believe that we will live for a few more years yet. We think it is other people who die – until it threatens to happen to us.

I realized impermanence when I saw the last breath of my father. This changed me irrevocably. I look at my family, myself, my friends in a very different light. I realized how human, how frail we all are. As Master Kusan used to say:

Our life rests upon a single breath.

When you are driving your car very fast to an appointment, is it better to risk dying, or to arrive late? When you have an argument with your partner over the washing up, would you feel differently if you recognized that he or she might die tomorrow?

Recognizing impermanence makes us realize that things can change. We have a tendency to fix, to 'permanentize'. We have a headache, we feel it will last at least a week. We have a problem, we tell ourselves it will last forever and become very anxious.

How are we going to stand this terrible thing, day in, day out? It is very rare for anything to last very long, be it our feelings, our thoughts, or even the world around us – everything changes constantly. If we accept that things change, then we open the door to an array of possibilities for ourselves and others. How often do we say: 'You are always like this! I am always like that!' This means that we must do that particular terrible thing twenty-four hours a day, seven days a week, etc. It would be very hard to sustain anything to that extent. As soon as a Zen student hears 'always', s/he questions this statement with wisdom: 'Is this true or even possible?' Ryokan writes:

> Time passes,
> There is no way
> We can hold it back–
> Why, then, do thoughts linger on,
> Long after everything else is gone?

LETTING GO

With the wisdom that comes from experiencing impermanence, we realize that lovers, friends, family, possessions, jobs, houses, etc, are only there for a short time and cannot give us lasting happiness; even if we are seduced by the hope that they will. We work very hard to achieve various things. We get a new car or a new job or a new lover. How long is it before frustration appears? Soon we find that the car is not going as fast as we had hoped or we are worried that somebody is going to scratch it. As for the new job, we feel that the atmosphere in the office is not pleasant enough after all, or the job is not as satisfying as we would have hoped. And if only your new partner would wash the dishes or be more romantic, then truly you could have it all and be happy.

It does not mean that we cannot appreciate and care for what we have but nothing can give us total, for ever, lasting happiness

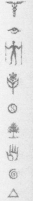

because we and they are impermanent and so unsatisfactory in terms of our hope for it. Understanding this will help us to strive less, to appreciate more and to be content with what is. Yunmen said:

Every day is a good day.

BEING ENLIGHTENED BY ALL THINGS

The final part of wisdom is understanding emptiness or non-self. Zen is not nihilistic, saying that everything is empty or that we do not exist. It is suggesting that we are not existing independently, separate from anything else and that inside us there is not a solid, unchanging kernel of something that is 'Me'. First, if we look at ourselves, can we say that since we were born there is something within us that has never changed? Imagine being a two-year-old baby, then a thirty-year-old adult, then sixty years old. How many changes in body, mind and speech have happened in these sixty years. Where is this constant, unchanging self?

We are an endless flow of conditions. The conditions are particular and definite because of our specific parents, genes, history, social circumstances. These conditions are unique to us. There is therefore a relative sense of self, but this is not constant nor can it be reduced to one state or thing. We have so many roles (mother, daughter, teacher, friend, customer, etc), so many different feelings and moods (happy, sad, elated, anxious, tired), how could we be just one thing? Even physically, one day we are tired and unwell and we look awful, another day, preparing to go out to a party, we look beautiful and radiant. The idea of non-self does not negate ourselves but actually helps us to discover how multi-faceted we are, how many possibilities we contain, how much there is to discover and uncover.

Realizing emptiness is to see that nothing exists separately or independently from anything else and therefore there is nothing to grasp. Again, looking at ourselves, who are we? Why do we feel so separate, so cut off? This is a strange delusion. We are totally interdependent with the whole world. For example, when we breathe, the world is constantly entering through our nostrils, our mouth and our pores into our body. We are not hermetically sealed. Furthermore, when we are with other people in a room, we are breathing the same air, their outbreath goes into our lungs and vice-versa. How much more intimate can we be!

Other things we depend on are food, clothes and shelter. Without these things we could not survive. So we are dependent on all that supports our life; in turn, these things – food, for example – depend on something else for them to be. Reading this book, you might be sitting on a chair. What is this chair? What makes it a chair? Where is the chairness of the chair, the self of this chair? Is it in the back, in the legs, in the cushioned part? Without any of the parts it is not a chair but any part by itself is not the chair either. It becomes a chair when all the components are put together and we sit on it. When the chair is in the way, we kick it and think it is a terrible chair. When we are tired, the chair is luxurious and soft and we think it is a wonderful chair. Terrible one minute, wonderful the next – what is the true state of the chair?

We do the same with people. We attach qualities to this imaginary, solid self and say: 'Claudia is good, John is bad', and generally 'for ever after' is implied. They might have certain tendencies but it is likely that they will be good or bad according to their own circumstances and our own preferences. The teaching on emptiness is trying to tell us that things and people are not as solid or as separate as we think they are. It is also trying to make us look beyond our simple assumptions and one-sided ideas in order to see a much bigger picture, and finally to grasp less and appreciate more. Dogen expressed this succinctly:

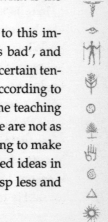

The way of the Buddha
Is to know yourself,
To know yourself
Is to forget yourself,
To forget yourself
is to be enlightened by all things.

THREE ATTITUDES: GREAT FAITH, GREAT COURAGE AND GREAT QUESTIONING

Great Faith, Great Courage and Great Questioning are the three qualities one is encouraged to cultivate in Zen practice. All Zen masters have expounded on them, but especially Tahui, Chinul and Hakuin. You find many references to these great qualities in their writings.

THE SUN IS SHINING BEHIND THE CLOUDS

Great Faith is faith in our own potential as Buddha, not in something outside of ourselves. Many different reasons might bring us to Zen practice: a friend, a teacher's talk, a book, a search for spirituality, and so on. As we begin to sit, in the quietness and clarity of the meditation, we realize that it is like coming home. There is a certain ease and simplicity. We start to have more faith in ourselves and in our potential.

When I was translating for Master Kusan in Korea, all kinds of people would come to visit him and I would often be there to help and to translate. Every time, whether they were Koreans or Westerners, young or old, farmers or historians, he would ask them exactly the same questions and give them the same instructions. This perplexed and disappointed me a little. I was hoping for more variety and spontaneous eloquence from a Zen master. Until I realized how beautiful and what a lesson this was! He truly believed that anyone could practise this method and become awakened. There was no need to embellish anything. He showed me Great Faith in action. He had Great Faith in the Buddha-nature of every single person; the Buddha-nature is not different in anybody, so why should his instructions be different? However, *his* Great Faith was not enough, because when we listened to his words, *we* had to have the Great Faith *ourselves* for it to work.

Great Faith might come upon someone suddenly, but generally it grows with practice. At the beginning, it is more like a belief and we feel rather separate from it. But as we continue, we see some changes in ourselves, we stop grasping so much at details, we open to possibilities, and peace and clarity become more familiar. We see ourselves better, we start to have faith in ourselves and the Zen practice. When suddenly we have some insight like Master Huangpo, we realize that this is not special, just our natural way of being. As he said:

> When at last in a single flash, you attain full realization, you will only be realizing the Buddha-nature which has been with you all the time.

However, now our vision is screened so we have to practise, but this practice is sustained by the Great Faith. It is like the sun being covered by thick clouds, we do not see the sun but we know it is there and it will appear again. In the same way, our intrinsic Buddha-nature is covered by delusions and ignorance, but they too come and go. The great faith will sustain us both when our practice goes well and when it does not. So the Great Faith is the basis and the ground for Zen practice.

GREAT COURAGE

We need Great Courage to continue on the path Great Faith has taken us upon. For example, Korean Master Hyobong used to

sit on a frozen river so the fresh air would keep him awake as he meditated for days and nights. Master Kusan used to sit on the edge of a cliff to keep himself alert when he meditated. I met a Zen nun who had been in silence for ten years to help her be less distracted in her meditation practice. All this requires Great Courage, but nobody told them to do this, they were inspired by Great Faith and determination.

What kind of courage do we require in this modern world with its complexities and urgencies? We need the courage to live in the present and not in the past or in the future. We need the courage to break our habits and patterns of thought. We need to let go of our preferences, impulses and desires. We have such a tendency to be lost in our negative thoughts or our hopeful dreams, or to give in to despondency or laziness. When we do this, we are creating strong habits. How can we change this painful behaviour? We actually need Great Courage to stand firm when we are buffeted by recurring desires, depressive thoughts, negative resentments or beautiful daydreams. We must come back again and again to *this* moment and to the practice of being quiet and clear in awareness.

There are two stories often used to demonstrate how our habit patterns limit us. Once there was a frog sitting peacefully by the side of a river. A scorpion came by and asked her urgently: 'I really need to go to the other side of this river, I cannot swim, can you take me across please?' The frog was dubious, she felt the scorpion was going to sting her. But he promised he would never do this as it would be senseless, as both would die in the middle of the river. So the frog, out of compassion, acquiesced. They started across the river, the scorpion on the back of the frog. Half way across, the scorpion stung the frog and as they both went down, the frog asked: 'Why did you do it?' 'I could not help it, it is in my nature', replied the scorpion. How many times do we do this? We know something is not a good idea, we are going to be hurt but out of habit we carry on doing it. Only Great Courage can help us to break through these very ingrained habits.

The second story is about an island inhabited by many monkeys. The islanders catch the monkeys by hanging coconuts with sweets inside them. The monkeys, attracted by the sweet smell, put a hand through the hole in the coconut and catch the sweets but cannot get the sweets or their hand out because the hole is too small. If a monkey lets go of the sweets, he can get his hand out and be free, but he wants the sweets, so he holds on and is then captured. It is the same with us: something is enticing so we hold onto it; through the holding we might experience pain but we cannot let go because we want it so much or it seems so attractive. Again we need Great Courage to look beyond the seduction and remember our intention to let go of suffering and to benefit ourselves and others.

For example, we think Zen is a great idea and that meditation is beneficial, but time and again we will find that we have time for everything else but meditation. From a Zen perspective, Great Courage would remind us of our faith in our Buddha-nature, of our vow to seek enlightenment for the benefit of all, and would help us to go beyond our limits. We might try to sit for thirty minutes instead of ten, and every morning instead of once a week. We might try to attend a week's retreat to see if we can do that. During my first three-month Zen retreat, I did not think I could cope and would often escape the schedule until Master Kusan noticed it and told me I had to bear beyond strength. I thought that if everyone else could do this, maybe I could give it a better try and within a month, I would be the first one to arrive. Great Courage will give us the impetus to go beyond our small habitual self and reach out to our wider potential for quietness and clarity.

GREAT QUESTIONING, GREAT AWAKENING

Great Questioning is traditionally called Great Doubt as in this Zen saying:

> Great Doubt, Great Awakening,
> Little Doubt, Little Awakening,
> No Doubt, No Awakening.

Doubt can mean vacillation in English. In Zen, doubt means questioning. If we want to awaken we need to produce a Great Doubt or Questioning in order to go beyond our usual concerns and anxieties, misconceptions and delusions.

There is a paradox between Great Faith and Great Questioning. We need faith to anchor us and questioning to open us. With faith only, we might stagnate and become narrow-minded, with questioning only we might become disturbed and agitated. These two qualities balance and support each other.

The Buddha strongly emphasized questioning and knowledge born of direct experience. Some villagers once asked him whose teachings they should follow. He told them they should question and test any teachings or practices that were presented to them. If the practices helped them to become more kind and wise, they should continue to practise them; if the practices made them more selfish and aggressive, they should try something else. We need to question anything that is presented to us, even Zen.

In Zen, we are invited to see life as a question. We are encouraged to open to the 'don't know' mind and to embrace the insecurity of uncertainty. This does not make us confused; on the contrary it allows us to wonder at life like a child and to find marvels in the most ordinary. This is not an intellectual enquiry, we need to be engaged with the whole of our being. It is said that we have to question with the marrow of our bones and the pores of our body. Dogen, asking himself how the Buddha-nature could be represented, thought that the only way it could be expressed was through the question: 'What is this?'

Master Kusan used to say that we needed to question meditation itself. We had to be careful not to grasp at any states, good or bad, and to maintain a balance between quietness and clarity. If we were too quiet we might become dull, so we needed to introduce more enquiry. If we were too focused on enquiry we might become agitated and would then be encouraged to bring more concentration into our meditation. He said we needed to be like hens hatching eggs. The hen moves the eggs at the bottom of the pile – the ones which are cooler – to the top and then moves the top ones down to the bottom so they all have an even temperature. We usually like to know just what to do and then do it, but in this way meditation can become mechanical. Great Enquiry or Great Doubt prevents this and keeps the practice fresh and lively.

In Zen, we are encouraged not to lose our beginner's mind, to be open and to avoid becoming too professional. For example, Master Chaochou, after being a revered master for many years, left his temple to travel on his own as a simple monk. His intention was to continue his training by learning from anyone he met, whether it was a five-year-old child or an illiterate farmer.

Master Chaochou (J: Joshu) was one of the great Chinese Zen masters who contributed much to the development and the characteristics of Zen in China. He had a long fruitful life and he died at the age of 120. He is well-known for his enigmatic answers to the various convoluted questions of his many disciples. For example:

A monk asked Chaochou: 'The myriad things return to one. Where does the one return to?'

Chaochou answered: 'When I was in Ch'ing Chou I made a cloth shirt. It weighed seven pounds.'

* Note on transliteration: Zen names and traditional words are generally written in Chinese ideograms which are pronounced slightly differently in China, Korea and Japan. Throughout the text, Chinese names or words referring to Chinese Zen will be written with the Chinese pronunciation and the same for Korean and Japanese names and words. Words such as Zen, Rinzai, Soto, Zazen, Koan which are better known in the Japanese pronunciation remain the same throughout the text. C: indicates the Chinese pronunciation, K: indicates the Korean pronunciation, and J: indicates the Japanese pronunciation.

2

HISTORY

Z en was developed in China after Buddhism entered that country in the first century CE. Buddhism was a foreign religion brought from India to China by merchants and travelling monks. Over the centuries the Chinese made Buddhism their own and transformed it in various ways. Many different Chinese Buddhist schools arose. The Zen school was the one that survived successfully the tribulations of Chinese history and was transmitted to Korea and Japan. At the root of Zen is Buddhism and the Buddha's life and teachings.

FROM BUDDHA TO BODHIDHARMA: A SPECIAL TRANSMISSION

The Buddha was born in India 2500 years ago. According to the legend, he was born a prince with great riches and lived within the precincts of a vast palace. However, in his late twenties, he left the palace four times to see the world. There he saw a sick person, an old woman, a dead man and a mendicant. These encounters confronted him with his own mortality and frailness. He realized that suffering was inescapable. He then decided to leave his palace and his wife and young child and become a mendicant to find an answer to the predicament life, old age, sickness and death presented to him.

After six years of adhering to different spiritual practices under various teachers in his search for an answer, he finally sat down alone under a tree (which became known as the *Bodhi* – enlightenment – tree). Six days later, still seated in meditation, at dawn he saw the morning star and awakened.

After his awakening to the origin of suffering and its cessation, the Buddha taught for many years. The Buddha's core teaching is that there is suffering. The origin of suffering is craving. The cessation of suffering is attained by eliminating craving and there is an eightfold path which leads to the end of suffering. The eightfold path is right view, right motivation, right speech, right action, right livelihood, right effort, right mindfulness and right concentration.

After the Buddha died, Buddhist monks and nuns spread his message and methods across India and bordering countries. As already stated, Buddhism reached China in the first century CE. There it met already established systems of philosophies and religions: Confucianism and Taoism. The first task was to translate the Buddhist texts into Chinese. Through this endeavour, over many centuries Buddhism became quite scholastic. It is thought that as a reaction to these scholarly tendencies Zen Buddhism arose with an emphasis on meditation and experiential wisdom achieved through direct awakening. An episode of the Buddha's teaching has come to be known as the first Zen story, although it predates the establishment of what is known as Zen.

One day, the Buddha was giving a talk to a great assembly of monks, nuns and laypeople. At one point, he held up a flower, displayed it to the crowd and remained silent. Only Mahakasyapa, one of his monk disciples, understood his meaning and smiled. The Buddha smiled back.

This is considered the first Zen transmission between master and disciple. Twenty-seven other Indian Patriarchs followed until the Indian monk Bodhidharma. Bodhidharma is reputed to have come as a monk from India in 479 to transmit the Buddhist teachings to China. After a long journey, he reached South China where he met Emperor Wu (502–550).

> Emperor Wu asked Bodhidharma how much merit he had accumulated by building many Buddhist temples and giving sumptuous offerings to the monasteries. Bodhidharma replied that he had created no merit whatsoever.
>
> Emperor Wu was perplexed by this reply and asked: 'What is the highest meaning of the holy truths?'
>
> Bodhidharma answered: 'Empty, without holiness.'
>
> The emperor said: 'Who is facing me?'
>
> Bodhidharma replied: 'I don't know.'

After this episode Bodhidharma is supposed to have crossed the Yangtse river on a reed and reached the kingdom of Wei. There he went to a mountain cave near Loyang where the Shao Lin temple was later erected. This temple has been made famous by Kungfu (martial arts) films which purport that Shao Lin style Kungfu was started here by Bodhidharma. Bodhidharma sat in a cave for nine years facing a wall. To this day, in the Shao Lin temple there is a stone in which the form of Bodhidharma is supposed to be embedded as he sat in front of it for so long.

Buddhist scholars have questioned many of the legends about Bodhidharma and even questioned whether or not he existed. The consensus seems to be that Bodhidharma should be seen more as a religious myth than as an historical figure. Scholars have also suggested that much of Zen history was created over two centuries (650 to 850). It served the purpose of giving legitimacy to the traditions and to inspire future generations.

This is not considered a cause of concern by most practitioners. For example, once the Western monks and nuns at Songkwang temple in Korea complained to Zen Master Kusan that many Zen stories were historically untrue. The master replied that it did not matter. For him, their truth did not depend on historical accuracy. Moreover, they had served the practitioners well over the centuries by helping them to be provoked, inspired and awakened.

These words attributed to Bodhidharma are the most often cited as representing the spirit of Zen.

> A special tradition outside the scriptures
> No dependence upon words and letters;
> Direct pointing at the heart of man,
> Seeing into one's own nature, one attains Buddhahood.

Early on, the Zen tradition claimed to be outside the scriptural tradition of the sutras, the recorded teachings of the Buddha, and commentaries about them. The practice was said not to require explanation. The only thing one had to do was 'to turn the light back onto oneself' in meditation and through that see one's own true nature. In doing so, one could be awakened and become a Buddha. Despite its insistence on direct experience Zen has produced as many texts as any other Buddhist tradition. Throughout the centuries, however, meditation has remained the main emphasis.

CHINESE CHAN: A SUDDEN TEACHING

After Bodhidharma, Zen transmission went on to Huiko (*c* 485–*c* 553). Huiko is said in the *Gateless Gates* (a record of encounters between masters and disciples) to have stood for many days outside the cave of Bodhidharma in the snow, imploring him to become his teacher. Finally he is supposed to have cut off his arm to prove his sincerity. (Scholars found that actually Huiko's arm was cut off by bandits and he had impressed everyone by remaining equanimous, which might be the reason why this incident is incorporated in this Zen story). Bodhidharma relented and asked him what he wanted.

> 'Your disciple's mind is not at peace. I beg you, master, give it a rest.'
>
> Bodhidharma said, 'Bring your mind to me and I will put it to rest.'
>
> Huiko sat for a while looking for his mind, then he said: 'I have searched for the mind but have not been able to find it.'
>
> Bodhidharma said, 'See, I have put it to rest for you then.'

This exchange resulted in the awakening of Huiko.

The theme of a restless mind is recurrent in Zen. We feel our mind is agitated or confused. We find ourselves burdened by this agitated mind. We keep running around, busying ourselves with stories about the past and the future, worries about what we have done or what we have to accomplish. However, if we just stop and look 'now' deeply into ourselves and our mind, we realize there is nothing *there* to be grasped. This experience can be very liberating.

Little is actually known of Huiko and the next two patriarchs Sengtsan (dates unknown) and Taohsin (580–651). One text, *Verses on Faith in Mind*, attributed to Sengtsan, presents in a long poem one of the main ideas of Zen, non-duality. The first verse says:

> The great Way is not difficult
> For those who have no preferences.

It raises this challenging question: how would our life be if we did not have such strong likes and dislikes? In Zen, we endeavour to realize that we are very attached to what we like and very eager to get rid of what we don't like. We begin to see that this pattern is causing us a lot of suffering.

Taohsin was followed by Hungjen (600–674), who was well-known in his time and had many disciples in his monastery on Mount Huang Mei. It is with one of his disciples, Huineng (638–713), that Zen became established as a distinctively Chinese form of Buddhism. There is a well-known story about Huineng and Shenhsiu, who both vied for the transmission of the patriarch's robes and bowl.

Hungjen felt his end coming so he gathered his disciples and told them to write a poem to express their understanding in order to know who to give the transmission to. Shenhsiu wrote:

The body is the Bodhi (enlightenment) tree
The mind is like a clear mirror
At all times we must wipe it clean
And must not let the dust collect.

However Huineng wrote:

Bodhi originally has no tree
The mirror also has no stand
Buddha-nature is always clean and pure,
Where can dust alight?

The first poem tells us that the mind is like a mirror and Zen practice is to keep it clean and free of dust. The second poem tells us that originally the mind is pure and bright, there is no place for the dust to rest and the practice is to know this.

The Zen tradition declares itself to be a sudden teaching. But over the centuries a debate has raged as to the suddenness and the gradualness of awakening and practice. Are practice and awakening both sudden or is there a gradual practice followed by a gradual enlightenment or is there a sudden awakening followed by gradual practice? Most Zen schools advocated suddenness and accused others of gradualism. The second poem is about sudden awakening and practice, and Huineng reportedly won the contest and became the Sixth Patriarch.

After Huineng, the teachings branched out and there started to be various lines of transmission, many of which continue to this present day. Each Zen master has a transmission booklet that has been given to them by their teacher when their awakening is recognized and 'sealed'. This process is called receiving 'Inka' (Dharma Seal). The booklet traces the line back generally all the way to the Buddha through the twenty-seven Indian Patriarchs and the six Chinese Patriarchs and the various Zen lines in China, Korea or Japan.

Huineng's *Platform Sutra*, in which his life and teachings are described, had a great influence on the Zen tradition. It is thought that Shenhui, his main disciple, compiled it and championed it so well that what is called the Southern teaching of Huineng eventually triumphed over the Northern School, led by Shenhsiu, the disciple of Hungjen who wrote the gradualist poem.

From 700 CE onwards, various schools of Zen arose which came to be called the Five Houses. Each contributed something to the taste of Zen. The Kueiyang sect is said to have been rough and hearty, preferring action and silence. If a master asked a question, his disciple had to answer with a deed. It also perfected the technique of drawing a circle as a way to describe enlightenment. The Fayen sect brought the technique of repeating the same word or phrase in answer to any question. The Yunmen sect brought the pass of a 'single word' as Master

Yunmen (died 949) was wont to reply to any spiritual questions, especially profound ones, by very few words.

> A monk asked Yunmen: 'What is talk that goes beyond Buddhas and patriarchs?'
> Yunmen replied: 'Cake!'

Only the last two schools, the Linchi (J: Rinzai), and the Tsaotung (J: Soto), survive to this day. The Linchi School is named after Master Linchi (died 866) who was renowned for his shouts and his hitting style. For example, once he was asked:

> 'What about the cardinal principle of the Buddha-dharma?'
> Master Linchi gave a shout.
> The monk bowed low.
> 'As an opponent in argument this young reverend is rather good,' the master said.

These Zen shouts are called Katsu. They are used to wake up the students to their own Buddha-nature instead of being lost in conceptualization or theories, by bringing them back to the experience of this very moment.

From the Linchi School came the tradition of the koans (C: Kung an, K: Kongan) which are test cases used in Zen meditation practice. There are 1700 koans which are compiled mainly in *The Gateless Gate* and *The Blue Cliff Record*. These are records of encounters between Zen masters and their disciples where often the master says something enigmatic which the student has to resolve by questioning without using the intellect. These encounters provoke the student to awaken by stopping the discursive mind and opening to one's own nature.

The Tsaotung School advocated the unity of relative (that which has to do with ordinary life) and absolute (that which has to do with the transcendent or awakened life). This unity was developed through several stages called the 'Five Ranks'. The fifth rank suggested a total unity which transcended all opposition which was often depicted in the image of a full black circle. This led the school to practise 'Silent Illumination', that is 'just sitting' without doing anything. Just sitting was considered enlightenment itself. There was a certain rivalry between the Linchi School and the Tsaotung School; the former accused the latter of being quietist, and the latter accused the former of being caught in words.

During the Tang Dynasty (618–907), Zen developed and its practical and radical nature helped the school survive the tribulations of Chinese politics. The Sung period (960–1297) saw an expansion and an artistic flowering of Zen. However, in the following centuries, with the revival of Confucianism and Taoism and the arrival of Vajrayana Buddhism from Tibet, Zen lost some of its importance and support.

Later on, Zen was influenced by the Pure Land School. This school was founded in 402 by the Chinese monk Huiyuan who stressed the importance of the mythical Buddha of light Amitabha who resides in a Pure Land known as the Western Paradise. The objective of the Pure Land believers is to be born in this Pure Land to be in the presence of Amitabha Buddha. Huiyuan devised the simple practice of reciting the name of Amitabha. As the position of Zen weakened in China, the practices of reciting the name of Amitabha and of questioning koans were amalgamated into the question: 'Who is reciting the Buddha's name?'

At the turn of this century, Master Laikuo was well known for his fierceness in directing retreats and his incisive comments. He would say:

You should know that the rules during a meditation week are severe and different from the usual rules. Today you take leave of

life and death before all the patriarchs, and before me. Now your life rests totally in these two hands of mine. If I want you to live, you'll live; if I want you to die, you'll die.

Many people are reputed to have gained insight on his retreats.

Master Hsuyun (1840–1959) was another outstanding representative of the Zen tradition. He lived to 120 and walked on pilgrimages all over China and even all the way to India. Many of the present-day Chinese masters are his disciples or part of his lineage. He was attacked by the Red Guards during the Cultural Revolution and many Zen monasteries and nunneries suffered greatly during that period. For the last twenty years Zen training has been allowed again and many monasteries are being rebuilt and repaired so that Zen monks and nuns are able to live a traditional Zen way of life anew.

KOREAN SON: A SYNCRETIC VISION

Buddhism entered Korea in the 4th century CE and in the following centuries five Buddhist doctrinal schools came into being. The Avatamsaka and the Popsong schools were the most influential on the future development of Zen in Korea as they prepared the ground on which Zen would grow. The Avatamsaka School took its name from the *Avatamsaka Sutra*, a Buddhist text which emphasizes the interpenetration of all things and teaches that Buddhas and sentient beings are the same. The Popsong (Dharma-nature) School was founded by Wonhyo, one of the most original thinkers in the history of Korea. His approach was syncretic as he tried to create a sense of unity among the various trends of Buddhist thought at that time.

Wonhyo had a dramatic awakening as a young monk. On his way to China to find a teacher and learn more about Buddhism, he had to rest at night in a field after a tiring day. Everything was dark and he was very thirsty. Groping around on the ground he found a bowl containing water. It was fresh and thirst quenching; it tasted like nectar. The next morning when he woke up, in daylight he saw that he had slept in an old tomb and actually the bowl had been a shattered skull filled with stagnant water. He was shocked and repulsed.

In that moment he realized that:

> ... thinking makes good and bad, life and death. And without thinking there is no universe, no Buddha, no dharma. All is one, and this one is empty. There is no need now to find a master.

One moment, the water was nectar and the bowl a saving grace; the next moment both were repulsive. He then decided he did not have to go to China after all and turned back.

During the emergence of Zen in China, Koreans had been in constant contact with many of the leading Chinese Buddhist figures. Zen finally reached Korea around 630. The first significant Korean Zen teacher was Toui (*d*. 825) who practised Zen in China for 37 years. When he returned to Korea, the various doctrinal schools, each of them based on a certain sutra or one special Buddhist theory, were very powerful and their influence too strong for him to make any headway. His Zen teaching was too unorthodox with its idea of not relying on words and doctrines. The doctrinal traditions emphasized the importance of studying the sutras and gaining a clear understanding of the Buddha's teachings. This new Zen tradition on the contrary put the emphasis on realizing the truth here and now through applying the Buddha's teaching by practising radical meditation.

After a while the simplicity and directness of Zen made it more popular and it was then that the influence of Wonhyo made itself felt. Instead of continuing the conflict with the doctrinal schools, a syncretic approach organically emerged where

the practice of Zen was provided with a solid theoretical under-pinning. The first teacher to try and harmonize the doctrinal and the Zen groups was Uich'on (1055–1101), the fourth son of King Munjong. He was only partly successful due to his bias against Zen. One hundred years later Chinul (1158–1210) succeeded in promoting an effective and enduring syncretic view. With Won-hyo, Chinul is considered the most influential figure in the history of Korean Buddhism. To this day, his many texts influence the life and practice in Korean Zen monasteries and nunneries.

In his *Admonitions to Beginning Students*, he writes:

> When the master goes up to his seat to preach the dharma, do not be overawed by it and, as before a steep precipice, turn away ... Listen to the sermon with an empty mind; then it will certainly be an occasion for you to attain enlightenment. Do not be like those sophists who have studied rhetoric and judge a person's wisdom only by his eloquence. As it is said, 'A snake drinks water and produces poison; a cow drinks water and produces milk.'

Chinul entered a monastery when he was seven years old. He became a novice at fifteen and successfully passed the clerical examinations at twenty-five. He could have pursued a monastic career but was appalled by the degeneration in the Buddhist institutions. So he went to the mountains to practise Zen and study the scriptures. He did not have a close relationship with any particular Zen master. What is striking about him is that during that time in retreat he had three separate awakenings, each triggered by certain passages in Zen texts he was reading: Huineng's *Platform Sutra*, Li Tongxuan's *Exposition of the Avatamsaka Sutra* and *The Records of Tahui*. Following these experiences, he decided to create his own community deep in the mountains away from the corrupting influence of the capital and the court. To one monk, he wrote this poem:

When the waves are choppy
It is difficult for the moon to appear,
Though the room is wide,
The lamp can fill it with light.
I exhort you to clear your mind-vessel,
Don't spill the sweet dew-sauce.

Chinul was convinced that there were no differences between the Buddhist sutras and the understanding that came from awakening through Zen practice. He developed and propagated the doctrine that he had found in the works of Tsungmi (780–841) of sudden awakening followed by gradual practice which is advocated today in many Zen monasteries in Korea. Chinul was also the first to introduce the huatou practice as devised by Tahui into the Korean Zen tradition. (The koan is the whole story of the encounter between a master and a disciple. The huatou is the crucial phrase which triggered understanding and then is used as a question, repeatedly asked in the practice.) However, his death at the age of fifty-two prevented him from officially and formally unifying all the various Zen and doctrinal schools.

T'aego (1301–82) was the next influential master in the Korean tradition. At an early age he was given the koan: 'Ten thousand things return to one; where does one return to?' When he was thirty-three, he experienced an awakening. As is the tradition he wrote a poem about this insight in which he wrote:

I drank up all the Buddhas and Patriarchs;
All the mountains and rivers,
Without my mouth.

Four years later, he experienced his final breakthrough and wrote:

After I break through a solid gate,
Clear wind blows from time immemorial.

This awakening was confirmed in China by Master Shihwu, an eighteenth-generation disciple in the line of Master Linchi. This made him the link in the line of transmission from China to Korea as Chinul was self-enlightened and not confirmed by anyone. T'aego was also important in unifying the Nine Mountain Schools of Zen which had developed over the centuries according to various lineages and had settled on nine different mountains all over Korea. This resulted in one single school, the Chogye Sect, so called after the mountain behind the main monastery of the Sixth Patriarch Huineng in China.

From 1392 until 1910, the Yi Dynasty took over from the Koryo Dynasty which had been very supportive of Buddhism. The Yi Dynasty was Confucianist and for the next 500 years various measures were enacted which repressed Buddhism. For example, from 1623 onwards Buddhist temples could not exist in the capital and monks and nuns were forbidden to enter. For this reason, today most major Zen monasteries and nunneries in Korea are situated in beautiful locations in the mountains. In 1910, Korea was occupied by Japan, a country more open to Buddhism but which brought over the concept of married 'monks'. After independence and the Korean war, the celibate monks of the Chogye Order regained control of most of the major Zen monasteries. The married monk T'aego Order is more associated with chanting and study.

One of the outstanding Zen masters at the turn of the century was Kyongho (1849–1912). On his travels, he was struck by a notice at the entrance of a village which declared: 'Danger: Cholera. If you value your life, go away.' He was terrified and recognized his limitations. He was humbled that even after he had read so many Buddhist sutras he could still be afraid. This inspired him to work on the koan: 'Before the donkey leaves, the horse has already arrived'. Since he felt that he was 'as good as dead' he decided he would not leave his room until he had gone beyond life and death. Finally, one day, through a student mentioning a cow with no nostril, he had a deep insight and wrote this poem:

> I heard about the cow without nostrils,
> And suddenly the whole universe is my home.
> Yonam Mountain lies flat under the road,
> A farmer, at the end of his work is singing.

He had a great influence in reviving the spirit of Zen in Korea through his teaching and his practice. Awakening at thirty-two, he taught until he was fifty-three and became well known and respected. Then he retired to a village, wore layclothes and grew his hair long. For nine years, he followed this simple way of life, instructing anyone he happened to meet.

Quite a few of his disciples became great Zen masters who in their turn helped to foster the continued revival of Zen in this century. The most prolific was Mangong (1872–1946) who had 25 Dharma heirs, and among them four nuns. One of his monk disciples, Kobong (1890–1961), was rather unorthodox in that he drank wine (which is forbidden by the monks' rules in Korea) and preferred to teach nuns and laypeople as he found the Zen·monks too lazy. One of his own disciples is Master Seungsan (*b.* 1927) who is very active internationally, especially in America and Poland.

Today Zen in Korea is alive and well. There are many Zen monks and nuns, and new young ones are ordained every year. One of the characteristics of Korean monastic Zen is that monks and nuns are quite equal. They live in separate places but have the same functions, teachings, practices and positions. In order

34 to become a monk or nun, one has to be a postulant for six months to a year, then one takes ten monastic vows as a novice (male: Sami; female: Samini). Later one can be fully ordained as a monk (Bikku) or a nun (Bikkuni). The monks observe about 250 vows and the nuns about 330. These ordinations have been transmitted from the time of the Buddha from India and Sri Lanka through China to Korea. After the first ordination, one generally goes to study sutras and Zen texts for three to four years in order to get a good grounding in the basic teachings of Buddhism and Zen. Following this period of study, one can join a Zen hall to practise meditation.

In the Zen hall, there is a formal schedule of regular practice in summer and in winter for three months each. The monks and nuns sit for about ten to twelve hours a day, rising at three or four and going to sleep at nine or ten. They sit for four periods during the day. Each period contains two, three or four meditation sittings of fifty minutes each and walking for ten minutes in between sitting, inside the hall. Every fifteen days, there is a bath and shaving day followed the next day with a lecture by the Zen master and the recitation of the vows by the whole assembly. Autumn and spring are free seasons during which the monks and the nuns can visit various temples and Zen teachers. In Korea, there are also many associations of laypeople who practise and study Zen.

JAPANESE ZEN: THE TRANSMISSION CONTINUES

In 552, Buddhism was introduced into Japan from Korea. Dosho was the first Japanese monk to be influenced by Zen when he went to China around 654 and upon his return built the first Zen hall in Japan. In the next two centuries, some Chinese Zen masters came to Japan and had a certain following. However, there were other schools of Buddhism in Japan which had a much stronger influence on the religious life of the country at that time, so Zen did not become popular and remained in abeyance for the next three centuries. It was during the Kamakura period (1185–1333) that Zen rose to prominence. Eisai (1141–1215) is considered the founder of the Zen tradition in Japan.

Eisai became a Buddhist Tendai monk in his youth. The Tendai School is a syncretistic Buddhist school developed in China which tries to harmonize all the Buddhist teachings and is based on the Lotus Sutra which contains the essential teachings of Mahayana Buddhism. Eisai visited China twice where he was struck by the spirit of Zen. On his second visit he received the Dharma Seal (Inka) in the Rinzai tradition and was in conflict with Tendai monks on his return as he started to teach Zen.

He built the first temple of the Rinzai (C: Linchi) sect in Japan, Shofuku-ji. However as a result of his own training, his teaching was flavoured by Tendai and Shingon ideas. The Shogun Minamoto Yoriie who was supportive of Zen because its rigour and strictness appealed to him, nominated Eisai as abbot of Kennin-ji monastery in Kyoto in 1204. This temple became the first monastery in Kyoto where Zen was taught above any other Buddhist teachings. It is here that Dogen met Eisai.

Dogen (1200–1253), the founder of the Soto (C: Tsaotung) Zen tradition in Japan is one of the more important Buddhist figures in that country. He became a monk at the age of thirteen and again like Eisai began his career by being trained in the Tendai School. However, he could not get an answer to this essential question:

If all beings originally possess the Buddha-nature, why does one need to engage in practices to realize it?

Someone suggested he went to China to study in the Zen school in order to find an answer. First he went to some temples where they studied the koans but he felt they put too much emphasis on illogical actions and words while discarding the deep meaning of the Buddhist sutras. He was going to give up and return to Japan when he was sent to Master Juching (1163–1228). A fierce, uncompromising monk, Juching eschewed fame and material trappings and objected to Zen being presented as 'a transmission outside the scriptures'. He also believed that the Great Way was not concerned with inside or outside and that Zen was 'dropping away body and mind', that is: forgetting our body and mind, not being so attached to our ideas, pains and pleasures. He taught zhigandazu (J: Shikantaza) as a form of meditation. As one sat, one did not try to answer any questions or riddles nor try to gain awakening.

Dogen's understanding was confirmed and he received the Dharma Seal from Master Juching. About this momentous event, he said:

> I was able to enact this face-to-face transmission by dropping away body and mind, and I have established this transmission in Japan.

He returned in 1227 and in the next few years wrote many of his important works such as *Instruction for the Tenzo (Head Cook)*, which are still followed in temples all over Japan, and started to expound some of the fascicles of *Treasury of the True Dharma Eye (Shobogenzo)*. From the Tendai headquarters on Mount Hiei there came opposition to his increasing popularity, so in 1243 he moved to Echizen Province where he founded Eihei-ji, which is still one of the two main monasteries of the Soto Zen school. Dogen died at the age of fifty-two in 1253 while visiting Kyoto for treatment of a serious illness.

Dogen put great emphasis on the posture while one sat in meditation and ascertained that sitting still, Zazen, was enlightenment itself. He said:

> The Buddha's way is under everyone's heel. Immersed in the way, clearly understand right on the spot. Immersed in enlightenment, you yourself are complete.

Sitting still, one is quiet but at the same time also bright and clear, but the mind is not moving, resting in 'non-thinking'. In a *Recommended Mode of Sitting Meditation* he writes:

> Think of what does not think. How do you think of what does not think? It is not thinking.

Unfortunately Dogen was nearly forgotten, even in his own school, over the centuries until he was rediscovered in the 1800s.

After his death, the political situation in Japan was full of strife until 1603 when Tokugawa became the Shogun (military ruler). During that time, Rinzai Zen fared better than Soto Zen as it appealed more to the warrior classes (samurai). Zen also became associated with various arts (Do) like the tea ceremony (Chado), archery and haiku writing. One of the popular Zen figures of these times is Zen Master Ikkyu (1394–1481), an iconoclast who was a great painter, calligrapher, poet and tea master. There are many stories told about his unconventional life. He liked to write about the decline of Zen and the enjoyment of wine and love.

> Who among Rinzai's descendants really transmits his Zen?
> It is concealed in this Blind Donkey.
> Straw sandals, a bamboo staff, an unfettered life –
> You can have your fancy chairs,
> meditation platforms, and fame-and-fortune Zen.

His poems reflect that in the course of the 15th and 16th centuries the Zen schools degenerated and Zen monks were mainly interested in keeping up form and appearances. Zen study became a secret oral transmission influenced by Shingon Buddhism. This school of Esoteric Buddhism was founded by the Japanese monk Kobo Daishi in the eighth century. It believed that the Buddhist teachings could not be explained and practised with words but with images and put a great emphasis on practising with mandalas (symbolic representations of an enlightened world).

The experience of enlightenment became formalized and lifeless. When the Tokugawa Period (1600–1867) started, people realized the damage created by the secret oral transmission and abandoned it, and searched for ways to revitalize the Zen tradition. One of the most original masters was Bankei (1622–1693) who, instead of harking back to the ancients and the koans, encouraged people to simply 'listen to the unborn Buddha-Heart'.

> A peasant once asked him: 'As a farmer I am absorbed in my chores and find it difficult to follow the Buddha-heart. How can I follow the unborn heart?'
>
> The master replied: 'Since all men possess the unborn Buddha-heart from their birth, you are not now seeking for the first time to follow it. If you perform your chores with all your might, you are practising the unborn heart.'

Bankei was extremely popular because he spoke in very ordinary, direct and comprehensible language, using a lot of his own experiences and mistakes. He contributed greatly to the revival of Zen in his time among the masses but had little to do with Zen institutions.

A few decades later Master Hakuin (1689–1769) reformed and revitalized the Rinzai tradition. All lineages of the Rinzai masters in Japan today come down from Hakuin. Hakuin created a koan system in which one first had to go through the gate of the koan 'Mu' ('No!') to provoke the first of several awakenings which followed an intensive study of a series of koans graduated by difficulty. He created the well-known koan, 'what is the sound of one-hand clapping?'. He also emphasized the importance of a well-regulated monastic atmosphere within which work was seen as an integral part of Zen practice.

> For penetrating to the depths of one's own true self-nature and for attaining a vitality valid on all occasions, nothing can surpass meditation in the midst of activity.

He reaffirmed the practice of Zazen as essential for Zen practitioners and wrote a defining poem on the subject, *Hakuin Zenji's Praise of Zazen*, which is still chanted in Japan today. He was also very concerned about the common people and endeavoured to find easier ways, like telling stories of miracles, to present Buddhist practices, which would be more accessible than a strict monastic Zen training and so would be beneficial to a wider audience. He was also a painter, calligrapher and sculptor. He was not really a trained artist but made wonderful and amusing caricatures of Bodhidharma, himself and also Kannon, the Bodhisattva of Compassion.

In the Soto tradition, Manzan Dohaku (1636–1714) tried to stop the abuses in the transmission of offices which had crept up and achieved notable improvements. With Gesshu Soko (1618–1696) and Menzan Zuiho (1683–1769), he was part of a group of reformers who endeavoured to abandon any references to Satori (enlightenment) and discourage the use of the koans. Their influences can be felt to this day in the Soto tradition.

The Tokugawa period, like in Korea at that time, was very influenced by Confucianism and the Zen sects were restricted in

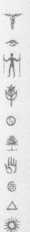

their activity by very strict state control. One of the notable Zen masters of the later Tokugawa period was Ryokan (1758–1831). He was a monk of the Soto school who received the seal of confirmation after studying for 12 years with Master Kokusen. Ryokan is famous for his poetry and for his life of great simplicity and indeed often of poverty. He is inspiring for his gentleness and acceptance of any circumstances, and his appreciation of beauty in all things.

> Without a jot of ambition left
> I let my nature flow where it will.
> There are ten days of rice in my bag
> And, by the hearth, a bundle of firewood.
> Who prattles of illusion or nirvana?
> Forgetting the equal dusts of name and fortune,
> Listening to the night rain on the roof of my hut,
> I sit at ease, both legs stretched out.

In 1868, there was a coup d'etat which restored the imperial regime, called the Meiji Restoration. The imperial powers were very nationalistic and established Shintoism as the state religion. They did not trust Buddhism partly because it was a foreign religion. They started to secularize Buddhism by encouraging monks to marry and to eat meat. Nowadays most Zen monks are married and generally inherit the familial temple from their fathers. One of their main duties is to chant at various services for their parishioners, especially funeral ones. These monks experience rigorous Zen training only for two or three years in the main monastic institutions in order to get their priest's certificate. The main training temples for the Soto School are Eihei-ji and Soji-ji, and Daitoku-ji and Myoshin-ji for the Rinzai School.

One of the important Japanese masters of this century is Kodo Sawaki (1880–1965) of the Soto tradition. Many Zen centres in the West have been influenced by his teaching. At the turn of the century a new lineage was created by Master Daiun Harada (1871–1961) and Hakuun Yasutani (1885–1973) in which both the Soto and the Rinzai Zen teachings were combined. In their system, disciples had to pass through various series of koans before they could start practising the Shikantaza of Dogen. Through their teaching in the West and their disciples settling there, their tradition has a major place in Western Zen.

RINZAI AND SOTO

RINZAI: THE WAY OF THE KOANS

LINCHI'S SHOUTS

The Rinzai (C: Linchi, K: Imjae) School takes its name from Master Linchi (died 866). He became a monk when he was a boy and started by studying Buddhist texts. However, as he became older he felt the need to put all these teachings into practice and experience enlightenment for himself. He went to practise Zen under Master Huangpo. After three years, he finally gathered the courage to visit him in his room. He went three times and was hit three times and could not understand why. Dejected and baffled he went to see Master Tayu who told him that actually Master Huangpo had treated him with great kindness and he was rather thick if he could not understand. Suddenly he saw the whole situation differently and had an awakening. Later he became famous for his abrupt style of teaching.

> A monk asked: 'Master, of what house is the tune you sing? To whose style of Chan do you succeed?'
>
> The Master said: 'When I was staying at Huangpo's place I questioned him three times and he hit me three times.'

The monk hesitated. The Master gave a shout and then struck him, saying: 'You can't drive a stake into empty sky.'

Linchi tried to lead his students to awakening by suddenly taking them out of their habitual patterns of action and thoughts through hitting them, roaring at them, surprising them. We often have a tendency to cruise along mechanically, and only a sudden jolt will bring us back to the true experience of this moment. At other times we are seduced by a train of thought, speculations and fabrications which can be enjoyable but have very little to do with being alive and awake in this instant. A roar from Master Linchi could wake us up from this conceptual dream.

Linchi also said:

> Attainment is attained instantly with no time required, no practice, no realizing, no gain, no loss ... For the Chan School, understanding is instantaneous, not a matter of time! All I teach is just temporary medicine to cure a corresponding illness.

He was a strong advocate of sudden awakening. For this reason, he tried to provoke it in his students by whatever shocking means. He knew it was there, he was trying to help it burst through.

He encouraged his students to keep their practice simple and not make it special or separate from the world they inhabited.

> Followers of the Way, as to Buddha-Dharma no effort is necessary. You have only to be ordinary with nothing to do – defecating, urinating, putting on clothes, eating food and lying down when tired ... The true student of the Way does not look to the faults of the world; he eagerly desires to seek true insight. If he attains true insight in its perfect clarity, then, indeed, that is all.

PRINCIPLES OF ZEN

There is an earthiness, a robustness to his teaching which marks the Chinese Linchi tradition to this day.

CHAOCHOU'S 'NO!'

At the time of Linchi there were many other great masters who also influenced the Rinzai school. One of them was Master Chaochou (778–897, J: Joshu, K: Joju). He experienced a profound awakening at an early age and following that, trained for many years under his teacher before wandering all over China to deepen his understanding. When he was eighty he settled in a small Zen temple in the town of Chaochou from which he took his name. He is responsible for one of the essential Zen koans, 'Mu' ('No!').

> After having given a talk in which he said that every sentient being had Buddha-nature, Master Chaochou returned to his room. A monk followed him; as he crossed the courtyard he saw a dog. The monk asked Master Chaochou: 'Does a dog have Buddha-nature, or not?' Chaochou replied: 'No!' (C: Wu, J: Mu, K: Mu).

All these encounters between Zen masters and disciples were compiled and started to be used as a training method in the Rinzai school. Master Tahui, for example, suggests: 'Whether walking, standing, sitting or lying down, just constantly call the story to mind: 'Does a dog have Buddha-nature or not? "No!".' But he advises us to be careful: 'Whether you're happy or angry, in a quiet or a noisy place, you still must bring up Chaochou's saying "A dog has no Buddha-nature". Above all, don't consciously await enlightenment. If you consciously await enlightenment, you're saying, "Right now, I'm deluded".' So in the Rinzai tradition one is asking a question unconditionally, without waiting for an answer and especially without waiting for an extraordinary experience.

In the Korean Rinzai tradition, as one questions the huatou (K: hwadu) 'No!', one is told to be careful of the ten diseases. The koan is the whole story and the huatou is the main question. Chinese and Korean Zen teachers use the term huatou more when talking about Zen practice and Japanese Zen teachers generally prefer to use only the term koan.

First, *'Do not entertain thoughts of "is" or "is not", "has" or "has not".'* As one questions 'No!', one must be careful not to get caught by the words of the koan itself.

Second, *'Do not think that Chaochou said "No!" because in reality there is just nothing.'* One must not take the 'No!' of Chaochou as a statement about the nature of reality itself and believe it is telling one that everything is empty.

Third, *'Do not resort to principles or theories.'* Do not try to explain this 'No!' by using various speculations and theories. This 'No!' goes beyond any set principle.

Fourth, *'Do not try to resolve the huatou by making it an object of intellectual inquiry.'* One cannot resolve the huatou intellectually, by thinking about it this way or that way, by trying to find various intellectual answers. It must come from our own experience, from our own struggle with it and from the whole of our being.

Fifth, *'When the master raises his eyebrows or blinks his eyes, do not take such things for indications about the meaning of the Dharma.'* Although Zen masters and mistresses are to be respected, we must be careful not to give our own authority and wisdom over to them. We must avoid putting them on a pedestal or thinking that they are perfect, projecting spiritual importance on everything they do. Once Master Kusan was in America in a Zen centre and we were taking a stroll with a young American. Suddenly the young man stopped and exclaimed: 'Just now, Master Kusan made such a profound gesture, what did he mean by it?' I translated this to Master Kusan who replied that he had just brushed his cheek with his hand because a fly had settled there and was tickling him. Nothing too profound about that we both thought!

Sixth, *'Do not regard the skilful use of words as a means to express the truth.'* On the spiritual path there are a lot of lofty words being used, truth, liberation, enlightenment, etc, and people who are clever with words can use them to great effect. What is important is not how beautifully they speak. Do they have the experience of what they are talking about? Do they live it in their everyday life? Or is it just for show?

Seventh, *'Do not confuse a state of vacuity and ease for realization of the truth.'* After we have practised Zen for a while, we might experience a state in which everything seems to be empty. There is no feeling of 'I', nor of the world, nor of distracted thoughts, but there is no questioning either. We don't have any pain and are quite relaxed but the mind is quite dull. We must be careful not to sink into such a state and remember to bring up the huatou vividly again and again.

Eighth, *'Do not take the place where you become aware of sense-objects to be the mind.'* Turning the light back onto ourselves we are inquiring into who we really are in this moment. We must be careful not to stop at the mind that sees, hears, feels, etc. Before we see, hear, feel, what is the mind? This is what we are trying to awaken to.

Ninth, *'Do not just rely upon words quoted from the teachings.'* The teachings of the Buddha, the patriarchs or the ancient Zen masters are not an end in themselves. We are not trying to accumulate knowledge of their words. Words in themselves will have no effect. They are there to be applied and understood. They are tools. If you just look at a shop window full of cakes this will not fill your stomach when you are hungry.

Tenth, *'Do not just remain in a deluded state waiting for enlightenment.'* If you go to a Zen centre or a monastery and believe that

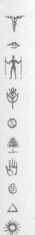

if you sit there long enough, you will imbibe enlightenment, it will not happen. We have to continuously inquire into the koan very deeply and assiduously. If we spend our time daydreaming in meditation or in daily life, we might develop imagination but we will not develop awareness, compassion or wisdom.

WHO IS REPEATING THE BUDDHA'S NAME?

As the centuries passed, the Rinzai tradition's fortunes waned and waxed in China where it was influenced by the Pure Land School. The practice in the Pure Land tradition is to recite the name of the Buddha Amitabha who is residing in the Pure Land. So the huatou practice of questioning and the practice of chanting Amitaba Buddha became one.

The silent, mental repetition of Buddha's name at all times and in all places serves to concentrate the mind and reduce distracted thoughts. The Chan masters adapted this technique and taught students to look at the mind which remembers to recite the name of the Buddha, turn their attention inwards on that place from where the thought is generated, and penetratingly examine the mind. The things that appeared before the meditator's eyes and ears were to be looked upon as illusory and impermanent; in the same manner the various thoughts and desires were also contemplated as unreal. When all traces of discrimination were wiped away and attachments abandoned, not even one thought would be produced and Buddha-nature would manifest itself brilliantly. Master Hsuyun explains:

> When one looks into a huatou, the most important thing is to give rise to a doubt. Doubt is the crutch of the huatou. For instance, when one is asked: 'Who is repeating Buddha's name?' Everybody knows that he, himself, repeats it, but is it repeated by the mouth or by the mind? If the mouth repeats it, why does it not do so when one sleeps? If the mind repeats it, what does the mind

look like? As mind is intangible, one is not clear about it. Consequently some slight feeling of doubt arises about 'Who'. This doubt should not be coarse; the finer it is the better. At all times and in all places this doubt should be looked into unremittingly, like an everflowing stream without giving rise to a second thought.

He points out:

All huatous have only one meaning which is very ordinary and has nothing peculiar about it. If you look into: 'Who is reciting a sutra?', 'Who is worshipping Buddha?', 'Who is sleeping?' The reply to 'Who' will invariably be the same: 'It is mind'. Word arises from Mind and Mind is the head of thought. Myriad things come from Mind and Mind is the head of myriad things. In reality a huatou is the head of a thought. The head of a thought is nothing but mind. To make it plain, before thought arises it is huatou. From the above, we know that to look into a huatou is to look into the Mind.

Later Rinzai Zen went to Japan, where it also had its own ebbs and flows. Finally, in the 17th century, it was in severe decline. Through the revival inspired by Master Hakuin (1689–1769), Japanese Rinzai Zen became quite different from its Chinese and Korean counterparts.

JAPANESE RINZAI: A SERIES OF KOANS

Hakuin wanted to come back to the strict koan study of previous times. He had undertaken koan study under many different teachers and this gave him a great knowledge of the koans and the methods used by various teaching lines. Hakuin himself had many deep awakening experiences (satori) and he wanted his students to strive for the same profound insight. He added some new elements and started to organize the koans into a course of study.

His method was to solve the koans through disciplined 'Zazen' (sitting meditation) combined with private interviews with the teacher. There was also the custom of adding verse comments taken from Chinese poetry to show one's understanding of a particular koan. Hakuin put the emphasis on the use of the koan 'Mu!' and also 'the Sound of the Single Hand Clapping' for the initial awakening which was to be followed by an intensive programme of koan study for the practice after awakening. Later followers Torei, Inzan and Kosen took his system and formalized it even more in a successive series of koans which had to be passed by the students in a particular order according to the level of difficulty.

There are generally five series of koans to master. The first are called Hosshin koans (ultimate reality). The aim of these koans is to show the first glimpse of the Buddha-nature and its unity and pervasiveness. Through working with them the student might experience his or her first breakthrough (kensho) and realize the oneness of all things.

> A monk asked Kassan Osho: 'What is the Dharmakaya?'
> Kassan replied: 'The Dharmakaya is without form'.

The next koans are called Kikan Koans (support). They are devised to help the student not grasp at unity but see the distinctness of reality.

> A monk asked Master Joshu: 'What is the meaning of Bodhidharma's coming from the West?'
> Joshu replied: 'The cypress tree in the garden'.

The next koans are the Gonsen Koans (pondering words). They are the words and phrases from the ancient masters that are difficult to understand. They help the students penetrate deeply into the meanings of the Zen patriarchs.

> A monk asked Nansen: 'Is there a truth that has not been preached to men?'
> 'There is,' replied Nansen.
> 'What is the truth?' asked the monk.
> Nansen answered: 'This is not mind, this is not Buddha, this is not a thing.'

The next type of koans are the Nanto Koans. Nanto means difficult to pass through. These koans are so difficult to resolve that the student needs to surpass him/herself. This supreme effort will enable the student to attain greater ease and insight.

> Goso Hoen Zenji said: 'It is like a water buffalo's passing through a window-lattice. Its head, horns and four hooves have all passed through. Why can't its tail pass through?'

The final stage is to penetrate the Goi (five) Koans which are also known as the 'Five Ranks'. The exposition of the five ranks is one of the main teachings of the Soto School. The Rinzai School contains some elements from the Soto School, in the same way that the Soto School, although advocating 'Silent Illumination', also makes use of the koans. At the beginning the two schools were quite close and their monks and nuns used to mingle in the same temple. However, over the next 200 years the two schools started to define for themselves a separate and distinct identity. Cultivating and passing through the 'Five Ranks' helps one to gain further insight and be without any grasping or delusion.

Although the Goi Koans are the ultimate in the series of koans to work through, this is not the end. One needs to continue one's practice by reflecting on how to live every day with great compassion and wisdom. So generally one continues with the study of the ten precepts (Jujukai), the five I mentioned in the first chapter (page 6) plus five others which are:

> do not discuss the faults of anyone among the four groups (monks, nuns, laymen, laywomen)
> do not slander another by praising yourself
> do not covet
> do not be stirred to anger
> do not revile the three Jewels (Buddha, Dharma and Sangha or Buddhist community).

Studying these precepts does not mean learning them by rote but investigating their meaning and their relevance to our daily life. The sixth precept about not discussing the faults of others, for example, is to remind ourselves how easily we might blame others, how their mistakes generally seem greater than ours and to look behind the action to the motive and the result. However, it does not mean that we should go around blindly letting people hurt others without saying anything. It is not a rule but a guideline that we learn to apply wisely and compassionately.

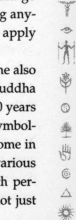

As one works in one's daily life with these precepts, one also reflects on the deep meaning of the three Jewels. The Buddha (first jewel) is not just the teacher who lived in India 2500 years ago, nor the golden statue which represents awakening symbolically. The Buddha is who we are right now and can become in this moment. The Dharma (second jewel) represents the various teachings of the Buddha but also the natural law which pervades the whole universe. The Sangha (third jewel) is not just the community of monks and nuns but anyone who aspires to enlightenment and displays compassion.

Working through the five series of koans and then on the precepts and the meaning of the three jewels is the sequence generally followed in the course of Rinzai Zen practice in Japan. In Korea and China, one would start with the precepts and respect for the three jewels and generally progress to work with only one koan. The main idea being that if you go through one you go through them all at once. Any koan can be the key to all other koans.

SOTO: SILENT ILLUMINATION

TUNGSHAN'S FIVE RANKS

The Soto (C: Tsaotung) School takes its name from its two founders who were master and disciple: Tungshan (807–869) and Tsaoshan (840–901). Tungshan became a novice in the Vinaya (Discipline) School of Buddhism. When he asked his teacher the meaning of a line in the *Heart Sutra*, his teacher could not answer. So Tungshan left to find an answer from the Zen masters of his day. He had his first enlightenment under the tutelage of Master Yunyen.

> Tungshan asked Master Yunyen: 'How should I describe your dharma if someone asks me about it after you have passed away?'
> Yunyen replied: 'Just say, "Just this is it!"' '

Master Yunyen taught him to understand the 'teaching given by inanimate things', to listen to the dharma talk given by a bird, presented by a flower. It does not require supernatural powers; on the contrary it is the awareness that we are connected to all things and that everything can speak to us about life, impermanence, emptiness, Buddhahood. Tsaoshan studied for many years under Master Tungshan who recognized his potential. After a while he decided to leave and wander on his own.

Tungshan said: 'Where are you going?'
Tsaoshan replied: 'To where there is no change.'
Tungshan asked further: 'How can you go where there is no change?'
Tsaoshan said: 'My going is no change.'

Tungshan explained the path of enlightenment through the 'Five Ranks'. The 'Five Ranks' are also known as the 'Five degrees' of enlightenment and express the relationship between the absolute or *Real* which represents emptiness, oneness, true nature, and the relative or *Apparent* which is concerned with form and colour, difference and various external qualities.

The first rank is *the Apparent within the Real*. Although the things of daily life dominate, one suddenly realizes that these emerge out of the absolute and that the relative is intimately connected and sustained by the absolute. Tungshan's verse for this rank is:

The Apparent within the Real:
In the third watch of the night
Before the moon appears,
No wonder when we meet
There is no recognition!
Still cherished in my heart
Is the beauty of earlier days.

At this level, one experiences a certain insight into the Buddha-nature and one really starts the practice. But one must continue to look deeper.

The second rank is *the Real within the Apparent*. There, oneness is preponderant and differences recede, one sees the ultimate in every single event, object, person, etc. The verse of Tungshan says:

> The Real within the Apparent:
> A sleepy-eyed grandma
> Encounters herself in an old mirror.
> Clearly she sees a face,
> But it doesn't resemble hers at all.
> Too bad, with a muddled head,
> She tries to recognize her reflection!

As Isshu Roshi explains: 'It is like mind and the objects of mind are one and the same; things and oneself are not two'.

The third rank is *the Coming from within the Real*. At this level, both body and mind drop away and one experiences emptiness.

> The Coming from within the Real:
> Within nothingness there is a path
> Leading away from the dusts of the world.
> Even if you observe the taboo
> On the present emperor's name,
> You will surpass that eloquent one of yore
> Who silenced every tongue.

Isshu Roshi suggests that 'in this rank the Bodhisattva does not remain in the state of attainment he has realized, but from the midst of the sea of effortlessness he lets his great uncaused compassion shine forth.'

The fourth rank is *the Arrival at Mutual Integration*. Everything is viewed in its respective individual form, its highest degree of uniqueness, one is fully aware of the world. Tungshan compares it to a lotus untouched by fire in the midst of fire.

The Arrival at Mutual Integration:
When two blades cross points,
There is no need to withdraw.
The master swordsman
Is like the lotus blooming in the fire.
Such a man has in and of himself
A heaven-soaring spirit.

In this rank, one is totally immersed in the world and responding fully to its demands but undisturbed by it, on the contrary inspired by its turbulences to greater height.

The fifth rank is *Unity Attained*. Form and emptiness interpenetrate. Ideas of awakening or ignorance disappear completely. Tungshan wrote:

Unity Attained:
Who dares to equal him
Who falls into neither being nor non-being!
All men want to leave
The current of ordinary life
But he, after all, comes back
To sit among the coals and ashes.

This is a state of complete non-attachment and freedom but still one is very much within the world, within this body.

JUST SITTING

The practice that emerged out of the ideas of the 'Five Ranks' is Mochao Chan (J: Mokusho Zen), that is the Zen of Silent Illumination. This expression and practice was introduced by Master Hungshi (1091–1157). Hungshi taught that awakening was to be experienced by sitting quietly, without focusing on anything special.

To learn the subtlety of Zen, you must clarify your mind and immerse your spirit in silent exercise of inner gazing. When you see into the source of reality, with no obstruction whatsoever, it is open and formless, like water in autumn, clear and bright, like the moon taking away the darkness of night.

Hungshi urges us to:

Just wash away the dust and dirt of subjective thoughts immediately. When the dust and dirt are washed away, your mind is open, shining brightly, without boundaries, without centres or extremes. Completely whole, radiant with light, it shines through the universe, cutting through past, present and future.

In this practice, the maintenance of a firm posture is important and the mind meditates upon its own stillness. The term Shikantaza (just sitting) was introduced and made popular by Dogen in Japan. 'Just sitting' means that the meditation is objectless and non-dualistic in that there is no specific object of concentration nor is one striving to achieve anything. One tries just to be, to exist and to be fully aware of that. Dogen believed that practice and enlightenment were one and the same thing.

Whenever a thought occurs, be aware of it, as soon as you are aware of it, it will vanish. If you remain for a long period forgetful of objects, you will naturally become unified. This is the essential art of Zazen.

But not only must one display the awakened state through sitting still but also in all activities. In *Instructions for the Cook*, Dogen says:

When you wash rice and prepare vegetables, you must do it with your own hands, and with your own eyes, making sincere effort. Do not be idle even for a moment. Do not be careful about one thing and careless about another ... Most of all you should avoid getting upset or complaining about the quantity of the food materials. You should practise in such a way that things come and abide in your mind, and your mind returns and abides in things, all through the day and night ... When you prepare food, do not see it with ordinary eyes and do not think with ordinary mind ... Do not arouse disdainful mind when you prepare a broth of wild grasses; do not arouse joyful mind when you prepare a fine cream soup. When there is no discrimination, how can there be distaste?

Dogen is encouraging us to bring a unified mind to all that we do. Practising daily means that we are totally present to our actions. Washing rice, the whole body/mind/heart must be present. We are aware of the colour, the smell, the coolness of the water; we are not somewhere else in our mind as our hands perform the action. We also wash the rice without discrimination, judgement or expectations, but with appreciation of the energy that was expanded to bring this rice to us and the benefit we will receive by being nourished by it.

Over the centuries, great emphasis was put on the importance of ritualized activities in both traditions, but especially the Soto school. Every activity becomes sacred as every action can display enlightenment. So rituals developed for making rice, entering and sitting in the meditation hall (Zendo), etc. These rituals were there to remind the Zen student of his/her intention, to be aware and awake. By coming back to the form of the ritual and its spirit one remembered the possibility of enlightened gesture in every moment.

The Soto tradition also put great importance on the respects due to the previous Zen teachers and patriarchs who have transmitted the teaching. So daily in Japanese Zen temples there is a ritual recitation of the names in the lineage all the way back to Shakyamuni Buddha.

TEN OXHERDING PICTURES

The Ten Oxherding Pictures describe the path to enlightenment and self-development in the Zen tradition. A series of poems and commentaries on the poems are also connected to them. You can see these pictures adorning the walls of Zen temples in China, Korea and Japan. It is the representation in folk images of the training of the mind, body and heart in Zen practice. They depict a young oxherder searching for and taming an ox.

1. SEARCHING FOR THE OX

High mountains, deep waters, and a dense jungle of grass –
However much you try, the way to proceed remains unclear!
To alleviate this sense of frustration, listen to the chirping of cicadas.

In this picture, the young oxherder is in nature looking a little lost, running here and there. He is searching for something but he is not even sure what he is looking for. This represents the stage when we have not started on the spiritual path yet but we feel somewhat uncomfortable and unsatisfied. There are faint stirrings within us.

We think that if we had enough material things we would be happy. We would like to have a house with a nice garden or enough money to buy whatever takes our fancy. But nothing seems to completely satisfy us, to bring us that elusive long-lasting happiness. Even indulging our senses completely through collecting art, taking drugs or going on holidays to beautiful places does not seem to work. We are still getting ill, ageing and near to death.

Perhaps we hoped that a good relationship would give us lasting happiness, but it is very hard to find the right person or be the right person, all-loving, all-accepting. Even if we find someone, we discover that one person cannot satisfy all our needs, wishes and hopes. A worthwhile or highly-paid job might give us meaning or security but again this covers only a certain period of our life. All these things give us only a fleeting happiness. It never lasts. Events keep happening which disturb our dream world. Something seems to be missing. We are like the oxherder in the picture, there is a refreshing stream, beautiful trees, colourful butterflies and wonderful birdsong but still he is not satisfied. Like us, he is anxiously looking for something, inner peace, contentment, clarity.

A tangle of thorny bushes: the faint murmur of running water.
But here and there are footprints – Is this the right path?
If you want to pierce its nose and tie it up, do not rely on someone else's strength!

In this picture, the oxherder finally see some footprints. It represents the stage when we decide to do something about the dissatisfaction. We look around for something. We discuss philosophy, read about psychology and various states of consciousness. We hear about meditation and Buddhism or Zen. We might have a friend who is practising or we might listen to a talk by a Zen teacher. We like the idea of liberation and awakening or the quirkiness of the koan 'What is the sound of one hand clapping?'. We find Zen poetry inspiring:

Silently a flower blooms
In silence falls away.
Yet here now, at this moment, at this place
The whole of the flower, the whole of
the world is blooming.
this is the talk of the flower,

The truth of the blossom
The glory of eternal life is fully shining here.

(ZENKEI SHIBAYAMA)

We are impressed by the peacefulness and clarity of the Zen teacher, we are attracted to the Zen stories but we stop there. We just read about it. It becomes part of our repertoire of ideas but we do not apply its tenets. So, very little changes, we continue to have the same sufferings, the same disturbing emotions and the same negative patterns. Reading or hearing about Zen only is not going to make a great difference in our life apart from bringing a certain exotic gloss. The other question this picture raises is: are the footprints old or new? Is this Zen teaching and meditation relevant to us now or is it only for ancient Zen masters in China?

3. SEEING THE OX

Among willow branches swaying in the spring breeze an oriole is singing.
How can the sparrow experience his joy in calling to his mate?
Isn't the moonlight glimmering in the forest my home?

In this picture, the oxherder finally sees the ox half-hidden among the trees. This image represents the stage where finally we decide to really do something. We are not totally sure yet what is the best method and what exactly we need to do. So we try various things. One week we visit a temple, another week we talk with a teacher. We continue to read books to find a good way to practise.

Finally, we might try Zen meditation and as soon as we sit down for a while we experience some peace. We realize that this is something we can do ourselves and it is beneficial. We might also try to cultivate the precepts and be more harmless, generous, disciplined, honest and clear. Again we see the point, we become familiar with the ideas not only at an intellectual level but also at an experiential level. We think that we have found something and we get very excited about it.

4. CATCHING THE OX

Advancing with difficulty; the ox's nose is pierced.
But this fiery nature is hard to control.
Dragged here and there, you stray through cloud-covered forests.

In this picture, the oxherder has finally caught the ox with a rope. But the ox does not want to be caught. The oxherder has to hang on tightly as the ox jumps fiercely and drags him hither and thither. We feel very much like the oxherder when we start to meditate. We are given a set of instructions and think that following them should not be too difficult. Catching the ox was not too hard but holding on to it definitely requires much energy and strength. In the same way, sitting down with a method is the easy part, while applying the instructions for a certain period of time is what needs great determination and strength.

As soon as we sit down with the aim of concentrating on the question or the breath or just being aware, our mind is flooded with thoughts, memories and plans and our body is not comfortable. We start to have pain in the back, then in the knees, then our cheeks start itching. We try various postures. We want to forget about the past or the future but they come back all the more quickly. Like the oxherder we have to be firm and hold on tightly. There are many obstacles: restlessness, sleepiness, daydreaming, etc. We have to realize that for the last twenty, thirty years we have cultivated many habits which promoted distractions and when we meditate we go against all these habits. It is going to take some time before we dissolve the power of these tendencies.

Sometimes the meditation goes very well and we have to be careful not to be attached to that ease because that too is impermanent – even though as we continue to practise the sense of ease lasts longer and happens more often. Sometimes the practice is very difficult, nothing seems to work; the thoughts seem intractable and the sleepiness so heavy, but that too passes a little faster as time goes by.

Fearing that it may fall into a steep and perilous path,
You hold it tight with whip and bridle, and with the strength
of both legs firmly hold your ground.
Once past this critical moment, the ox comes following you.

In this picture, the oxherder is gently tending the ox and the ox
is not wild anymore. They are walking alongside each other and
the oxherder is holding the rope very loosely. After having held
on tight and sustained the practice for a while, it becomes easier.
We are more comfortable with the sitting posture. We can sit
still without feeling restless. We are not fighting with our body
and mind any more. We are more present and we can concentrate for a certain period of time. We have gained some quietness and clarity which helps us in our daily life.

The oxherder is still holding on to the rope loosely because he
knows that although the fight is over, he must remain vigilant.
The ox seems subdued but it could jump off at any moment. To
practise Zen we have to be confident but aware of not becoming
arrogant. We might feel that we know all about Zen but we still
need determination and discipline as the powers of distractions
are strong. This picture represents a stage of maturation and
ripening accompanied by care.

6. RIDING THE OX BACK HOME

Sitting astride the ox, the noble person happily returns.
The sounds of his flute mingles with the crimson sky:
He has discovered the garden of joy.
Who else could know about this endlessly pleasurable taste?

In this picture, the rope has gone. The oxherder is sitting leisure-ly on the ox playing the flute. The ox knows where to go without being told. This is an image of ease, leisure and freedom. Some people believe that Zen is very strict and serious or that to be spiritual one has to be gloomy or indifferent. On the contrary, as we advance in the practice we find it is about joy and creativity. As we slowly release the attachment and grasping which used to create so much tension, laughter bubbles within us. We begin to take ourselves less seriously and enjoy life so much more as we open to its changing and ever-fluctuating nature. We dance and sing with life. We have become friends with our body and mind.

This picture also shows us that there is a place for creativity in Zen. As we accept ourselves and the world our potential unfolds, fears and insecurities dissolve and we can express ourselves creatively. It might be through music, painting, poetry, cooking, gardening, being with children or old people. Everything we do can become an art, it is not a duty anymore; it is a way to express our true nature.

Bright Moon and cool wind: what a splendid home!
Sitting all alone, the ox has gone away.
Even if you doze until sunrise, what use would be a whip and bridle?

The ox has disappeared and the oxherder is resting alone at home. Until now there was this idea that there was something to do, something to practise. There was a separation between ourselves and the practice. There was a dualism between what was spiritual and not spiritual, what was Zen and not Zen. At this stage, we become united with the practice. It is not special anymore. It does not happen just when we sit on a cushion in a special room. Everything becomes meditation.

Awareness becomes as natural as breathing. This is Zen in daily life. We take one thing at a time, fully present to it, and when we move we let it go without residue. We are at peace with ourselves, our mind, body and heart, with the whole world. We do not even need to try, to discipline ourselves, because now the practice and the cultivation of the precepts come unheeded. We do not have to do it, it does itself. As Master Kusan used to say: 'You are one with the question. It is the question that walks, goes to the toilet, looks at the countryside'. Harmlessness and generosity come naturally. In this state, you cannot even think of being unkind or telling lies, those kind of thoughts do not arise.

8. THE OX AND THE OXHERDER ARE BOTH FORGOTTEN

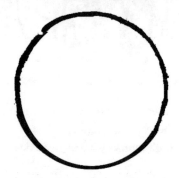

Since space has collapsed, how can obstacles remain?
Could a snowflake survive inside a burning flame?
You cheerfully come and go: how could you not always laugh?

The oxherder and the ox are both gone. There is only a black circle. It represents emptiness. Earlier, when we became united with the practice, there was this idea that it is 'me, I' that was practising. Until now there were strong notions of me, mine. Now this has gone too. We realize that nothing belongs to us truly, we can only care for it while it lasts. We also experience that we do not have a solid, separate identity. We are a flow of conditions. We are made up of all our genes, history, social conditioning, etc. Who are we but a bundle of aggregates and fluctuations? We cannot identify with our feeling, our thoughts, our possessions. They all come and go. They rise upon certain circumstances, stay a while and disappear.

Everything is made up of conditions which are ever-changing. There is nowhere to go, nothing to stick to. We realize that we are more than any of the parts that constitute us. The recognition that we cannot hold onto anything is a great liberation. A great burden is let go of. We feel so light. We realize that everything comes out of emptiness. Only because of emptiness can things change and flow. Emptiness is not a vacuum, a black hole, but the possibility of endless transformations. There is no more grasping, or self-created barriers and limitations. The Buddha-nature can shine through and express itself fully.

9. RETURNING TO THE ORIGINAL PLACE

My very own treasure is recovered: all those efforts spent in vain!
It would be better to have been blind, deaf, and dumb.
The mountains and water are just as they are!
So is the bird among the flowers.

In this picture, there is water flowing, flowers are blooming and birds are singing. The practice does not stop at emptiness. If we attach ourselves to emptiness it could lead to separation and isolation. So we have to go one stage further, re-entering the world where 'having forgotten ourselves, we are enlightened by all things'. We realize the interdependence which is at the

root of all life. When we are having breakfast in the morning, as we eat and chew a piece of toast we connect with the grain, the green shoots, the earth, the sun, the rain, and appreciate the efforts of all the people who made that piece of toast possible. When we see a blade of grass swaying in the breeze we are swaying with it.

Our life is ordinary and just as it is but we look at it differently. We realize that everything expresses the truth of life and awareness, and is talking to us. We do not skip on the surface of things any more but we are intimately related and experiencing every single item without grasping or rejecting. We are not locked in on ourselves anymore but fully open to the world. We are not frightened but on the contrary exhilarated. The world is us and we are the world. All this practice – just to realize what was on our very doorsteps!

10. ENTERING THE MARKET PLACE WITH HELPING HANDS

Ragged and bare-footed, you approach the market and the streets.
Even covered in dust, why would the laughter cease?
The bees and butterflies are happy because flowers have bloomed on a withered tree.

The picture shows a ragged, pot-bellied man walking barefoot bearing a sack full of goodies. This last stage represents freedom, wisdom and compassion. We are not encumbered by appearances. We adapt freely to high and low places. We find spirituality everywhere, it is not confined to monasteries and secluded places. Meditation and realization do not make us passive but active. We are deeply connected to the world, we feel its suffering and we want to respond and help. Our bag is full of joy, compassion, understanding, loving-kindness, wisdom and skilful means.

We naturally give to ourselves and others what is beneficial. We listen deeply, we observe unobtrusively and respond appropriately. When we give we do not expect anything. We are not superior to others when we help them, on the contrary helping them is like helping ourselves and we are grateful they give us that opportunity to extend ourselves. When we love it is with total acceptance. We do not help only people we like and who are easy to be with but also people who are difficult and grumpy. However, we do not force our ideas – our opinions, what works for us – on others. We try to bring lightness into people's lives. We do not take it all too seriously.

When we look at the Ten Oxherding Pictures we have to be careful not to think that self-development and Zen practice go in a straight line. It is more like a spiral. We go round and up, hopefully. We go back to different stages but with more understanding. We deepen our realization of each stage as we continue on the path. We still have delusions and attachments to shed. We discover more ways to develop concentration and enquiry further. Master Kusan had three different major awakenings, and each time he continued to practise even more. The last time, his own teacher, Master Hyobong, said: 'Until now you have been following me; now it is I who should follow you.'

5

ZEN MEDITATION
EXERCISES

The Buddha taught four postures to meditate in: sitting,
walking, standing and lying down. In formal Zen meditation, sitting and walking are specially used.

SITTING LIKE A MOUNTAIN

Sitting meditation is an art. In Zen practice, one might sit for
long periods of time repeatedly. Great emphasis is laid on main-
taining a good posture so the sitting is comfortable. Such a posture will help the mind to be clearer and the breathing to be
smoother and healthier.

We can sit in different postures. Traditionally these are the
full lotus posture and the half-lotus posture. In *A Generally Recommended Mode of Sitting Meditation*, Dogen wrote:

> Spread a thick sitting mat where you usually sit, and use a cush-
> ion on top of this. You may sit in the full-lotus posture, or in the
> half-lotus posture. For the full-lotus posture (Figure 1), first place
> the right foot on the left thigh, then the left foot on the right thigh.
> For the half-lotus posture (Figure 2), just place the left foot on the
> right thigh. Wear loose clothing and keep it orderly.

Next place the right hand on the left leg, and the left hand on the right hand, with palms facing upward. The two thumbs face each other and hold each other up.

Now sit upright with your body straight. Do not lean to the left or tilt to the right, bend forward or lean backward. Align the ears with the shoulders, and the nose with the navel. The tongue should rest on the upper palate, the teeth and lips should be closed. The eyes should always be open. The breathing should pass subtly through the nose.

Once the physical form is in order, exhale fully through the mouth once, sway left and right, then settle into sitting perfectly still.

Nowadays people also sit in quarter-lotus with the foot on the opposite calf, or in the Burmese style, or kneel on a cushion, or on a bench. One can also sit on a chair if one finds it difficult to sit on the floor. In the Burmese style (Figure 3), the left foot is not put on the right thigh but just in front of the right leg. Kneeling on a cushion (Figure 4), the legs are placed either side of the cushion; sometimes several cushions are used for that position. Kneeling on a bench (Figure 5), the legs are tucked under the bench; one might use a soft pad on the bench in order not to cut the circulation to the legs. Sitting in a chair (Figure 6), one sits with the back erect, half-way on the seat, trying not to lean against the back of the chair. One might put a cushion on the chair and sometimes a cushion under the feet. If one sits fully in a chair, with one's back touching the back of the chair, one must be very careful not to slouch and get into an unhealthy posture which would constrict the breathing and be harmful to the body.

1 Full-lotus: right foot on left thigh, left foot on right thigh.
Right hand on left leg, left hand on right hand.

2 Half-lotus: left foot on right thigh. Right hand on left leg,
left hand on right hand.

3 Burmese style: left foot against right lower leg on floor.
Right hand on left leg, left hand on right hand.

4 Kneeling on a cushion: legs on floor either side of cushion.

PRINCIPLES OF ZEN

5 Kneeling on a bench: legs tucked under bench.

6 Sitting on a chair: half-way on the seat if possible.

In all these postures, the traditional Zen way is to have the eyes half-closed to prevent drowsiness or agitation. The eyes are not fixed on anything but just gazing downwards at a forty-five degree angle. The back is straight but not rigidly so. The shoulders are comfortably low and the head rests lightly on the shoulders. The chin should be slightly drawn in. When sitting on the floor we are trying to form a triangle with the legs as the base and the head at the top so that we feel stable and grounded but relaxed at the same time.

The hands are on each other, palm up as instructed by Dogen and the thumbs are lightly touching each other. The hands are in front of the navel, the arms slightly apart from the body, and sometimes it helps to place a small towel or a thin cushion on the legs on which the hands can more easily rest.

We breathe quietly through the nose. We do not control the breathing but let it flow naturally. We try not to breathe noisily. Often it is recommended to breathe with the lower abdomen. It is suggested that it helps to make the breathing deeper. In this system, when one inhales the lower abdomen fills up, when one exhales it becomes concave; one also needs to be able to relax the diaphragm.

When sitting in half-lotus or the Burmese posture one does not need to always put the same leg on top or in the front. One can alternate the position of the right leg and the left leg. Generally, one sits on two cushions in the lotus, half-lotus or Burmese style: a rectangular flat pad or cushion (J: Zabuton) to make it more comfortable for the legs and a round cushion (J: Zafu) to get the right height for the bottom. Sometimes one might put some smaller cushions under the knees so one is more stable if both knees cannot rest on the Zabuton. In the kneeling postures one only uses the flat cushion (Zabuton).

WALKING WITH AWARENESS

Between sessions of sitting meditation (Zazen) one does walking meditation (J: Kinhin). There are various styles and speeds. In China, one walks clockwise around the Buddha statue in the meditation hall or outside in a circle, slowly, or at a steady pace, or fast with the arms hanging alongside loosely. In Korea one walks inside the meditation hall anti-clockwise but on the outer rim of the cushions at an ordinary pace with the arms relaxed and loose. In China and Japan, the cushions are situated closer to the walls and in Korea they are laid in two lines more towards the middle of the room.

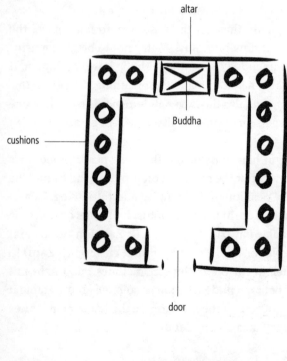

Japanese Zen hall

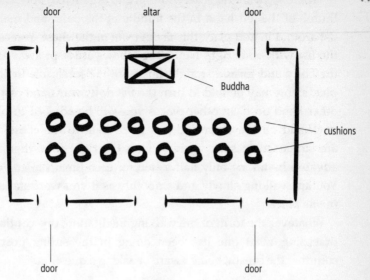

door   altar   door

Buddha

cushions

door   door

Korean Zen hall

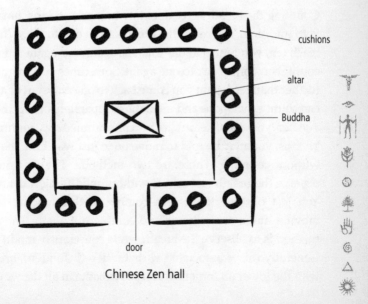

cushions

altar

Buddha

door

Chinese Zen hall

In Japan, the walking is very formal and organized. You put the thumb of the left hand in the middle of the palm and make a fist around it. You place this fist in front of the chest. You cover the fist with your right hand. The elbows are kept away from the body and form a straight line with the forearms. In some places you may be told to turn the fist downward and rest the other hand on it. In other places you will be advised to place one hand on the other and just hold them to the chest. You are supposed to start walking with the right foot, then you advance by taking only half a step for each breath in and out. You are walking slowly and smoothly as if you were standing in one place.

Whatever the form of the walking meditation, one continues practising what one has been doing in the sitting posture: counting the breath, being aware or asking a question.

COUNTING THE BREATH

Counting the breath is used mainly in Japan and in China in the Soto tradition. You count the breaths from one to ten. When you reach ten, you return to one and start counting again. If you lose count, you come back to one again. Sometimes you might count further than ten, again you come back to one and start again. You can count exhalations and inhalations separately or together.

After you have learnt to be concentrated by counting the breaths, you may be told to move on to just watching the breath without counting. There are two methods. The first one is to observe the breath just as it is without modifying it in any way. You just observe the breath coming in through the nostrils, moving down to the lungs and coming out again. The second method is to observe the breath while consciously modifying it. Generally this is associated with Tantien (J: Tanden), breathing with the lower abdomen. You try to breathe in all the way to the abdomen, then you might hold the breath very slightly for one or two seconds and then let it out again.

In the breath meditation, the breath becomes the object of concentration. Whenever you are distracted by thoughts, feelings, or sounds you try to come back as soon as possible to the breath. When counting the breath you realize quickly how distracted you can be. It is often difficult to count all the way to ten without thinking of something else. When you observe the breath, because you are very quiet, after a while the breath might become fainter. You should not stop concentrating then, but instead continue to observe gently but intently this subtle breath as there is no doubt that you continue to breathe no matter how faint it might be.

When first watching or counting the breath it might feel somewhat artificial and mechanical, because in paying attention to the breath you feel you are controlling it more. You need to relax and be confident, then you will become naturally attuned to the breath and become one with it. The question, 'who does it?' will no longer be important. In the end, the breath does itself.

JUST SITTING

In the Chinese Tsaotung tradition it is called 'Silent Illumination'. We sit quietly in a good sitting posture and are aware of the whole world and the whole of ourself in this moment. And the quiet brightness of the mind appears naturally as we remain still with no object of concentration but the sitting itself. Master Sheng Yen advises:

> You must be at a stage where there is no problem becoming settled, when you can sit with unbroken concentration, with almost no outside thoughts ... [Otherwise] It is hard to tell whether your

mind is 'bright and open' or just blank. You can be idling, having very subtle thoughts, and believe you are practising Silent Illumination. You can be silent without illuminating anything.

In silent illumination, there is a gradual stilling of the mind and thoughts slowly become less powerful and more intermittent. They become as light as bubbles, and as insubstantial as froth as the brightness of the mind shines more fully. Hongzhi said:

> Just expand and illuminate the original truth unconcerned by external conditions ... The deep source, transparent down to the bottom, can radiantly shine and can respond unencumbered to each speck of dust without becoming its partner ... Open-minded and bright without defilements, simply penetrate and drop off everything ... Immediately you can sparkle and respond to the world.

In the Japanese tradition, Dogen refers to the notion of Shikantaza, 'just sitting'. As Yasutani Roshi presents it:

> Shikantaza is a practice in which the mind is intensely involved in just sitting ... The correct temper of mind therefore becomes doubly important. In Shikantaza, the mind must be unhurried yet at the same time firmly planted or massively composed, like Mount Fuji let us say. But it must also be alert, stretched, like a taut bowstring. So Shikantaza is a heightened state of concentrated awareness wherein one is neither tense nor hurried, and certainly never slack.

Shikantaza requires intense concentration. Sometimes one sees pictures of Zen monks sitting in the snow. They are not cold because of the heat generated by this intense concentration. Often it is recommended not to do Shikantaza for more than thirty minutes at a time, as it is difficult for the body and the mind to keep up such a level of energy. Then one can do walking meditation for a little while and start again refreshed. At the beginning one might feel somewhat tense doing this practice, but after a while one can relax and rest in awareness without undue strain.

WHAT IS THIS?

In Korea one generally practises the koan 'What is this?'. 'What is this?' comes from an encounter between the Sixth Patriarch Huineng and a young monk who became one of his foremost disciple, Huaijang.

> Huaijang entered the room and bowed to Huineng. Huineng asked: 'Where do you come from?'
>
> 'I came from Mount Sung', replied Huaijang.
>
> 'What is this and how did it get here?' demanded Huineng.
>
> Huaijang could not answer and remained speechless. He practised for many years until he understood. He went to see Huineng to tell him about his breakthrough.
>
> Huineng asked: 'What is this?'
>
> Huaijang replied: 'To say it is like something is not the point. But still it can be cultivated.'

The whole story is considered the koan and the question itself 'What is this?' the hwadu (C: huatou). One sits in meditation and asks again and again 'What is this? What is this?' What is it that moves, thinks, speaks? Even more before we think, move, speak, what is this? We are not asking about external objects: what is the carpet, the cup of tea, the sound of the bird? We turn the light back onto ourselves: what is this in this moment?

We have to be very careful, this is not an intellectual enquiry. We are not speculating with our mind. We are trying to become one with the question. The most important part of the question is not the meaning of the words themselves but the question mark. We are asking unconditionally 'What is this?' without looking for an answer, without expecting an answer. We are questioning for its own sake.

We are trying to develop a sensation of openness, of wonderment. As we throw out the question 'What is this?', we are opening ourselves to the mysterious nature of this moment. We are letting go of our need for knowledge and security. There is no place where we can rest. Our body and mind become a question.

In terms of concentration, we are returning to the question again and again. The question anchors us and brings us back to this moment. But we are not repeating the question like a mantra. These are not sacred words and it does not matter how many times we repeat them. What is important is that the questioning is alive, that the question is fresh each time we ask it. We are asking because we do not know. It is similar to when we lose some keys. We look and look and look and we have no idea where they are and we cannot find them anywhere. Whenever we think about the keys we experience a sensation of perplexity that is not intellectual, just a feeling of not-knowing.

There are several ways to ask the question. At the beginning especially we can connect the question with the breath. We breathe in, then as we breathe out, we ask 'What is this?'. Otherwise we can try to make the questioning like a circle, we ask gently but steadily, as soon as one 'What is this?' stops another 'What is this?' starts. Once our concentration is firmer, we can just ask the question from time to time and stay with the sensation of questioning it evokes. As soon as the sensation of questioning dissipates we raise the question again, using the words vividly.

MU

In Japan one generally starts the study of koans by investigating the koan 'Mu!'. When Master Chaochou was asked if a dog had Buddha-nature, he said: 'Wu!'. This 'Wu!' is pronounced 'Mu' in Korean and Japanese. Some people take this 'Mu' as just an exclamation and when practising do not translate it. So the practice is to repeat inwardly the word 'Mu'. This is often associated with breathing from below the abdomen (tanden breathing). One tries to locate the Mu in the abdomen and become one with it.

Others translate the word 'Wu!' as 'nothing', 'without', 'no'. Then one is perplexed by this answer of Chaochou. The Buddha said that all beings have the Buddha-nature. So why did Chaochou say no? What did he mean by it? What was his state of mind before he said it? Then the practice becomes the enquiry of 'What is Mu?'. One continuously asks about Mu. One is perplexed by this Mu, one does not understand it, one does not know. Mu becomes a barrier that one has to pierce through. One cannot let it rest. Mu becomes like a mosquito trying to pierce our skin, infuriating. Yasutani Roshi said:

> Don't let go of Mu even for a moment while sitting, standing, walking, eating, working ... To become lax even for a second is to separate yourself from Mu. Even when you go to bed continue to absorb yourself in Mu and when you awaken, awaken with your mind focused on Mu. At every moment your entire attention must be concentrated on penetrating Mu ... You will become enlightened only after you have poured the whole force of your being into oneness with Mu ... Once you realize Mu, you know that nothing can be opposed to it, since everything is Mu ... In the intense asking, 'What is Mu?' you bring the reasoning mind to an impasse, void of every thought ... Trying to answer 'What is Mu?'

rationally is like trying to smash your fist through an iron wall ... Only through unthinking absorption in Mu can you achieve oneness ... Mu is beyond meaning and no meaning.

In this kind of enquiry, one has to be careful not to try to figure out Mu with the intellect. This is not an exam test in which there is one specific answer to a specific question. One is trying to experience Mu, not to think it. One is endeavouring to release the fixed mind with its set answers and definitions and open oneself to the world of experience which is flowing, spacious and in flux. After realizing Mu, a Zen student is said to have entered the 'world of Mu'. After this, one trains with various other koans, and Mu continues to be experienced and understood in deeper ways.

ON A RETREAT

I n the West generally Zen retreats are organized for a week
at a time. They are, in the main, held in silence. There are
some variations in the schedule and tasks according to the
teacher, the style, the school, the cultural background.

THE CHINESE WAY

A Chan retreat is quite an undertaking as it is about self-
confrontation and challenges one's habits and comforts. One
rises at four in the morning and goes to bed at ten at night. The
day consists of sitting and walking periods accompanied by
two sessions for work, such as cleaning, washing-up, cooking,
chopping wood, depending on what is deemed necessary. The
sitting sessions last a half-hour but participants may miss the
exercise break and continue until the next one if they wish and
have the capacity to do so. When there are a few minutes to rest
one is encouraged to do voluntary meditation or meditative
walking. One can also continue to sit late into the night. The
main rules of the retreat are silence, punctuality and tidiness.
A basic schedule goes as follows:

0400	Rising Clappers
0415	Exercises
0425	Tea
0440	Zazen: 3 periods
0630	Morning Chant
0700	Breakfast
0730	Work period
0830	Rest
0915	Talk by the teacher
1000	Zazen: 4 periods with short exercise breaks
1200	Lunch
1230	Work and rest periods
1415	Zazen: 4 periods with short exercise breaks
1615	Tea
1630	Evening Chant or mantras
1700	Zazen: 2 periods with break
1830	Supper
1945	Talk by the teacher
2045	Zazen: 2 periods with break
2200	Lights out

The meals are taken formally. Everyone eats together at the same table. The table is always set with a plate, a bowl, a glass, a fork, a knife, a spoon and a paper serviette. After the food is served, there is a blessing, then the food is eaten in silence. When everyone has eaten, water is passed around to clean the utensils which are then dried with the paper serviette. The cleaning water is poured into a bowl and another blessing is recited. After that, the bowl is taken to the place dedicated to the hungry ghosts and poured over it while reciting a special mantra connected to them.

There are three main reasons for cultivating silence on a seven-day retreat. The first one is that it helps the mind to

become calmer. As the input and output of words and conversation are severely diminished, there are fewer distractions for the mind to follow or to create. We do not have to find interesting things to talk about to impress other people, nor do we need to become involved in other people's various stories or ideas.

The second reason is to help us to accept ourselves and become friends with who we are. By being silent for seven days, we get to know ourselves intimately. We learn to appreciate ourselves and our inner potential. In the silence things become clearer and we realize the misconceptions and misapprehensions we can have about ourselves. We become friends with the ordinary human being who is alive, who breathes moment to moment, who longs for peace and clarity.

The third reason is to be with a group of people, to communicate and share with them in a different way. Although we do not speak to each other, we support each other by our mere presence and willingness to be there. No one is better than the next person, we are experiencing the same difficulties. By all sitting together with discipline and sincerity we are helping each other's practice and intention.

Master Sheng Yen teaches that the purpose of a Chan retreat is to:

1 Realize one is not in control of one's own mind.
2 Discover how to train the mind in awareness.
3 Calm the mind.
4 Provide opportunities for repentance and hence regain purity.
5 Practise with an individually suitable method that will yield insight.

Various methods are taught during a Chan retreat from watching and counting the breath to huatou practice and Silent

Illumination. Between sittings (Zazen) there is standing yoga, or sitting yoga, or slow and fast walking. The walking is in a circle either inside or outside.

Every morning and evening there is some chanting and repetition of mantras. The *Heart Sutra*, which is a text about emptiness, is recited twice a day. In the morning, one also chants the Ten Vows of Samantabhadra Bodhisattva, then the Four Great Vows and finally the Three Refuges. In the evening, one chants the Liturgy of Food Bestowal as an offering of spiritual food to all sentient beings. One finishes with the Three Refuges and a prayer of dedication to offer the merits of the retreat to others.

There are also talks given by the teacher. They can be formal commentaries on passages from ancient Zen texts or more practical instructions about the practice and the state of mind one is trying to develop. There are also private interviews with the teacher about one's personal practice or the difficulties one might have during the retreat or about the progress one is making. The teachers might admonish, question one's expectations, suggest practical ways to deal with certain problems, inspire one to greater heights, or intensify one's perplexity through direct Zen enquiry.

A MODERN KOREAN RETREAT

Certain Western meditation teachers adapt the Asian way of practising meditation to make it easier for Western students to attend. Normally in Korea one would get up at three in the morning and sit for fifty minutes at a time and walk for ten minutes ten to twelve times a day until nine or ten at night. This can be very difficult especially if one is not used to sitting cross-legged on the floor. Furthermore, although in Korea the ceremonies are reduced to a minimum compared to other Buddhist countries, there are still several throughout the day including formal meals.

In a modern Korean retreat, traditional aspects are reduced to the bare minimum but the essentials remain.

0615	Wake up
0645	3 Formal bows
0650	Sitting Meditation
0730	Breakfast (informal)
0830	Work period
0930	Rest
1000	Instructions
1030	Sitting
1105	Walking (inside the hall)
1115	Sitting
1150	Walking
1200	Sitting
1230	Lunch (informal)
1430	Sitting
1505	Walking
1515	Sitting
1550	Walking (free, outside)
1610	Sitting
1645	Walking
1655	Sitting
1730	Light supper (informal)
1900	Talk by the teacher
2000	Walking
2030	3 formal bows
2035	Sitting
2110	End of the day

During this retreat, as one is walking, sitting, standing, lying down, working, one tries to ask repeatedly and with great perplexity 'What is this?'. The times are not marked with the sound of a bell but with the clap of a 'Jukpi', a thin strip of wood cut in half, two-thirds of the way down. The 'Jukpi' is also used for the formal bowing.

There are three formal bows in the early morning and in the evening. Only people who are comfortable with Zen ceremonies need attend. The teacher lights some incense and a candle and pours some water in a bowl. The incense represents selflessness as it consumes itself at the same time as it gives fragrance to others. The candle represents light and wisdom. The water represents purity and flexibility as it adapts itself to all milieu. The three bows can be seen as paying respect to the three Jewels of the Buddha, Dharma and Sangha, or it can be seen as paying respect to one's own Buddha nature and reminding oneself that awakening is a possibility for everyone.

The instructions deal with the technical aspects of meditation like the various postures, the different obstacles one encounters and cultivating the right attitude to meditate more easily. The evening talks present the philosophy and the principles of the Zen tradition in a modern context. At the end of the talk, there is a question and answer session.

There are private interviews. At dedicated times, generally in the afternoon, as the meditation and walking session is in progress, the retreatants, one at a time, get up and see the teacher in a separate room for fifteen minutes. At the end of the interview, the person comes back to their place in the meditation room, and the person next to them gets up to go for their interview. The interview is to help the teacher to get to know the retreatants and answer any personal questions they might have about Zen or life in general.

On a Japanese-style retreat, the teacher might teach either the Rinzai or the Soto approach or both depending on the lineage they belong to. People are encouraged to wear black or dark-coloured loose clothes. If one becomes a disciple of the teacher and a follower of that specific group, one might wear Japanese-style Zen garb when on retreat: special loose black trousers or a wide black skirt and a black tunic or a special sitting robe.

Japanese Zen retreats are very formal with many directives on how to behave: how to eat the formal meal, how to enter and leave the Zen Hall, how to sit and walk. One enters the Zen Hall (Zendo) with the hands in the *shashu* position (formal walking meditation posture as described previously), stepping forward with the left foot on the left side of the door. One leaves stepping out with the right foot on the right side of the entrance. There is a formal way to go to your seat. When in front of your seat, you bow towards your cushion with the palms together (gassho). Then you turn around until your cushion is behind you and bow again in the opposite direction. Then you sit down on your cushion (zafu). There is also a formal way to leave your place.

A bell is rung to indicate the beginning and ending of the meditation period. When meditation begins, the bell is rung three times. When walking meditation starts, the bell is rung twice and when it finishes, once. When the sitting meditation (Zazen) ends, the bell is rung once.

During sitting meditation periods a person who walks around the room holding a stick will hit you on the shoulder to help ease tension in the shoulders, or sometimes if you slouch or nod, look sleepy or sluggish. In certain centres it is automatic; in other centres you are only hit if you request it. If you request the stick (kyosaku), you make a signal by putting the palms together as the stick holder (jikido) approaches. Then the stick is

placed on your right shoulder as you lower your head to the left. After being hit, you straighten your head again and bow. The stick holder also bows to you holding the stick with both hands.

The retreats are held in total silence and generally eye contact between the retreatants is not recommended. A regular schedule could be like this:

0400	Wake up
0430	Zazen (several periods of walking meditation are included)
0630	Ceremony
0700	Breakfast
0740	Cleaning
0800	Work period (samu)
0910	Preparation for meditation
0930	Zazen
1130	Ceremony
1145	Lunch
1230	Rest
1400	Zazen
1430	Talk (J: teisho) by the teacher
1530	Zazen
1630	Ceremony
1645	Dinner
1730	Rest
1830	Zazen
2100	Zazen ends
2130	Sleep

An important part of a Japanese Zen retreat is to go for interviews (dokusan) with the teacher several times during the week or even during one day. At the sound of a certain bell, people who want to have an interview will rush to a waiting room and wait there in the kneeling position. When another bell is rung, one strikes a prepared answering bell and proceeds to the interview. The retreatant enters the interview room very quietly and mindfully and exchanges bows with the teacher. The teacher might ask about the koan one is working on, or provoke one to an intuitive response about one's understanding, or discuss the difficulties one might be having. When the interview is finished, the teacher rings a bell and the retreatant leaves and the next person in line will enter. Many students look forward to these interviews and see them as a way to test themselves and their practice.

The talks are generally carried out in a traditional way by taking a Zen text and commenting on it. The teacher might describe a koan from the *Gateless Gate*, explain the various commentaries that were added to it throughout the centuries and make its teaching relevant to the particular retreat. The teacher will also conduct some ceremonies throughout the day similar to those on a Chan retreat, apart from the homage to the lineage which is specific to a Japanese retreat. The group intones the name of each master in the lineage, bowing at each name.

These Zen retreats are quite intense and are supposed to help us go beyond our small concerns, difficulties and attachments by pushing us beyond our limits. Sometimes students might experience some breakthrough or awakening (Kensho/Satori) and realize their Buddha-nature. This might manifest as everything becoming clear, or feeling at one with the universe, or realizing there is nothing to cling to and nothing to cling with. Sometimes people might feel elated or joyous or very light or totally free.

OBSTACLES

There are many difficulties one might encounter as one goes on a Zen retreat, especially at the beginning. The first obstacle we are challenged by is pain. It is not only the physical pain of sitting in one posture for thirty minutes or so cross-legged, but also the mental pain of being still for a certain period of time. One is not used to this. The physical pain improves over time. One can also do some stretching exercises like yoga to help limbs become more supple. But it is much easier to sit if one's mind accepts and experiences that there is nothing else to do at that moment. Then one can rest in stillness and clarity.

It is important to remember that everyone is different in mind and in body. It might be easy for someone to sit in full-lotus and difficult for someone else to sit in the Burmese position even with many cushions. One of the rules should be that if the pain disappears as soon as one stands up and walks then it is negligible. However, if the pain in the knees or ankles continues for some time one needs to find a different posture and combination of cushions and stool or otherwise just use a chair.

Some teachers insist on traditional zazen in half-lotus at least, some think it is more important for the mind to be concentrated on the question than to spend most of our time worrying about the pain. It is important to notice that the way we feel about any pain can depend very much on what is going on with our mind. If we are totally engrossed in daydreams, we do not feel any twinges. If we are concentrated, we feel relaxed and solid in the posture. Sometimes being at one with the pain can make it dissolve. However, we are on the whole half-concentrated and half-distracted so then we notice pain strongly, start to identify with it and worry: is my knee going to fall off? Will I ever walk again?

SLEEPINESS

Another obstacle is sleepiness or dullness of mind. As soon as we sit down we feel heavy and listless and start to nod. There, two things need to be considered. Did we work very hard before we came to the retreat? Are our body and mind excessively tired? Or is it that we feel fit and awake in other activities but when we sit we become very sleepy, yet as soon as the bell rings the end of the sitting we feel wide awake again. Then sleepiness arises out of escapism, not wanting to deal with ourselves and the intensity of the practice.

There are various remedies to this problem. The first one is to remind ourselves of our intention: Why did we come to this retreat? What inspired us to make that decision? Intention is a strong part of what will give impetus to our practice. The other thing we need to do is to observe our posture: as soon as we slouch, our mind will become dull. This is one of the reasons why so much emphasis is put on having a good posture in Zen. A straight, relaxed back will keep us fresh and alert. We might need to open our eyes wide for a few minutes to bring more light into our consciousness. If all else fails, we can remind ourselves that death is only one breath away. Would we be so sleepy if we reflected that we could die tonight or tomorrow?

BUSY BODY, BUSY MIND

Another obstacle is restlessness in the body and in the mind. First we feel we cannot sit still, we have pain in the knee, we have an itch in the lower back, we move this way and that way, and things only improve for a few minutes. We nearly feel like we are sitting on an ant heap. It is very important then to just sit still and relax into the posture and not give in to impatience. We need to rest in the moment, in the meditation and stop fighting.

When we begin to sit in meditation we realize with horror that our mind seems never to be still. It is running here and there to this memory, that plan, images, worries, dreams, grievances, desire for food or sex. It is very hard to stop this continuous agitation. Sitting still helps. The purpose of concentration is to slow down this ever-frenetic process. As we come back again and again with steadiness and determination to the object of concentration, our thoughts become less busy, we start to see the patterns of mind that keep us from being present.

We notice the tendency we have to daydream. This generally starts with the words: 'if I had ...', 'if I was ...'. In the daydream we are the actor, director, screenwriter, producer. We have total control over this imagined reality and it is extremely pleasant. We can spend hours doing this, meditation passes very swiftly then, we do not even notice if we have pain in our legs.

We might have a tendency to ruminate over some pain or hurt we have suffered in the past. As we sit in meditation, we'll go over the story again and again until we have had enough of that painful reminiscence and then move the ruminations to the future and plot revenge, going over which scenario would bring the most revenge and satisfaction. This habit will certainly not lead to more wisdom and compassion.

On a silent retreat it is easy to fabricate stories out of nothing or very little. The teacher or another retreatant seems to look at you funny. You wonder what is wrong with you and spin a great story about that. Then you might decide that actually there must be something wrong with them to look at you like that and you spin another story. In actual fact they probably just had a twinge in the stomach or some dust in their eyes.

Sometimes we have a tendency to plan. We plan how we are going to meditate later; how much we will eat at lunchtime; what we will do at the end of the retreat when we are finally enlightened; what kind of pension we should get for our old age. Or we judge fairly constantly: are we sitting well or not; is the teacher speaking well or not; is the person sitting next to you bowing properly. We have many such tendencies that we start to see more clearly as we meditate and as we concentrate we start to dissolve the power of these habits over our mind.

EXPECTATIONS

The higher the expectations we have of what a retreat will do for us, the less likely it is to happen. It is important to be inspired in order to achieve something. However, the more set the goal and the time to achieve it, the more pressure we will put on ourselves. Zen is about openness, not-knowing, questioning, looking freshly at the world and ourselves. We cannot fix and solidify what is unpredictable. The ancient Zen masters had their own experiences which are unrepeatable because each person's practice and set of circumstances are different. We need to let go of our desires even towards awakening and special experiences. What will happen will happen; just be sincere, determined and open.

Sometimes we might experience special states when we meditate intensely. We might feel ourselves dissolving. We might be without any grasping for a few minutes, totally at one with the question or 'Mu!'. We might experience bliss or a total open heart and love. We have to be careful not to grasp at these experiences and want to replicate them exactly again and again. They come, they nourish us, they show us that we can be different from what we generally think we are. By grasping at them and fixing them we stop ourselves from opening to even better experiences that we might never have dreamt about.

We also have to be careful when we leave the retreat not to grasp at that either. Your daily life situation is very different from the circumstances of a retreat in silence, with the guidance

100   of a teacher, with a certain discipline, the support of the group and long periods in meditation. We can continue to meditate daily but in a way which fits our circumstances, a little at a time throughout the day whenever there is a gap and nothing is happening. It is useful to continue to meditate formally for ten to thirty minutes a day as regularly as we can manage with our schedule and family. It can also help to join a sitting group once a week or every month to give us support, so we do not feel alone in our Zen journey.

ZEN AND THE MODERN WORLD

ZEN IN AMERICA

In 1987 there were under 200 Zen centres or groups in the United States and 10 years later there are more than four hundred. In the distant past there had only been awkward encounters between Zen and Christian missionaries in China and in Japan. The first real glimpse of Zen in the West occurred when Rinzai Zen Master Soyen Shaku was invited to speak at the World's Parliament of Religions in Chicago in 1893.

Afterwards he was asked to help with some translations and he recommended Daisetz Teitaro Suzuki, one of his young students. Through this, DT Suzuki (1869–1966) became one of the foremost exponents and writers of Zen throughout the Western world in the fifties and sixties. DT Suzuki tried to make sense of Zen for Western readers. He did not expound so much on the practical, technical aspects of the practice but more on the ultimate awakening or enlightenment, free from boundaries or religion. He inspired many seminal writers such as Eric Fromm, CG Jung and Aldous Huxley and poets including Allen Ginsberg and Gary Snyder. Alan Watts and others were also inspired to popularize Zen further and present it in a form accessible to everyone.

In 1905 Soyen Shaku returned to America as he was invited to teach Zen by a family in San Francisco. With him came his disciple Nyogen Senzaki (1876–1958), a free-thinking and unassuming monk, who was the first Zen teacher to settle in America. He started to instruct Westerners in Zen meditation in his 'floating Zendos', public halls he would rent whenever he had saved enough money from various small jobs.

Through him, Soen Roshi and his friend, Yasutani Roshi, and later on his disciple, Koun Yamada, came to America, which led to the introduction of the independent Sanbo Kyodan School, founded in 1954 in Japan. This school was created to offer a Zen which would be more open and accessible to ordinary people and in which the practices of Shikantaza and the Koans would be harmonized. Robert Aitken Roshi, one of the foremost American Zen Roshis, has been inspired by this school which designated a very important role to laypeople. Aitken Roshi himself is one of the most eminent writers and practitioners of Engaged Buddhism, as well as being involved in developing Zen ethics.

At the same time, there were many Chinese, Korean and Japanese immigrants coming into the USA and, in their wake, Zen monks to serve their needs. Taizan Maezumi Roshi was one of them. He first came to take care of the Soto Japanese temple in Los Angeles. In 1967 he went on to found the Zen Center of Los Angeles in order to train Westerners. Having received transmission in the Soto, Rinzai and Sanbo Kyodan traditions, he taught 'just sitting' as well as koan study. He gave transmission to twelve students who went on to create many different Zen centres all over America; the most active and well-known ones being Bernard Tetsugen Glassman, Dennis Genpo Merzel and John Daido Loori.

Shunryu Suzuki, the author of *Zen Mind, Beginners' Mind*, had also come to serve the Japanese community, at Sokoji temple in San Francisco. In 1969, he moved to 300 Page Street which became the San Francisco Zen Center. From this centre many new projects were initiated: a bakery, a restaurant, a farm training centre, a mountain centre, a Buddhist hospice movement.

Many Americans also went to Japan to train in Zen, or became attracted to the principles and practice of Zen while in Japan. Philip Kapleau Roshi is a good example. He was a court reporter for the International Military Tribunal in Tokyo after the war in 1947. He then trained in different Soto and Rinzai temples and studied with Harada Roshi, Yasutani Roshi and Nakagawa Soen Roshi. From all these experiences, he compiled and wrote the very influential Zen book *The Three Pillars of Zen*.

Now a new generation of Zen teachers is arising who have rarely been to Japan or studied with Japanese Roshis. Some of them are moving away from a very monastic lifestyle and trying to integrate Zen into a household life with work, family and varied relationships.

Recently, various scandals about sex, power and money have shaken various Zen centres and teachers, and made them reflect on democratic structures versus hierarchical ones, the responsibility and boundaries between teachers and disciples, and the relevance of the precepts to Zen practice. Certain Zen ideas, wrongly interpreted, might lead people to disregard the importance of the precepts in their training and daily life. This misinterpretation and the non-respect of ethics often create suffering and this is something that Western students of Zen have to consider and ponder.

ZEN AND WESTERN RELIGIONS

The Sanbo Kyodan School in Japan was created to open Zen and its practice to a wider public. This led to the inclusion of non-Buddhists. Also, the emphasis away from the monastics and toward laypeople took away the requirement of having to

ordain in order to train properly. Soon Christian monks and priests started to practise Zen as well. Father Enomiya-Lassalle, a German Jesuit priest, lived in Japan for many years during which he practised in Hosshinji and Sojiji.

He was acknowledged as a Roshi by Koun Yamada Roshi and more than twelve monks and priests were subsequently authorized to teach in the style of the Sanbo Kyodan School by himself and his successor Jiun Kubota, among them Willigis Jager and Ama Samy. These Christians did not have to become Buddhists to study Zen. They trained in 'Sitting still' and the study of the koans but kept their Christian religious context, the emphasis being on inner realization. Nowadays there are many Christian/Zen centres, especially in Germany, Holland and France.

Another connection between Christianity and Zen is monasticism. Since 1978, groups of Christian and Buddhist monks and nuns have gone to live in each other's monasteries for several months at a time, totally immersing themselves in the life of the other. A Benedictine monk reflected after one of these stays:

> The monastic ideal is a universal archetype. In all great religions we find men and women who seek to realize the unity of their persons and to reach original simplicity ... As we bade farewell, we realized that we had taken part in a rediscovering of separated brethren.

There also seems to be a connection between Zen and Judaism. Many of the Western teachers, especially in America, are from Jewish backgrounds. By becoming deeply involved with Zen practice, Western Zen students often rediscover their own religious roots, such as Judaism. Several books have been published about Judaism and Zen due to the deepening of the interest in their connection. Tetsugen Roshi, for example, is very supportive of religious dialogue with other faiths. Recently he

gave transmission to Rabbi Singer who was also ordained as a
Zen priest.

WOMEN AND ZEN

Japanese Zen has been very influential in Zen's development in the West. Traditionally, however, it is quite tough, strict and rather patriarchal. There are very few nuns or female priests in Japan and very few training places for them compared to those for men. Even though the monks were strongly encouraged to marry after the Meiji Restoration, nuns are not supposed to. It is only recently that the wives of male priests have been given any official status; until then their marriage was not recognized officially and their status similar to that of concubines. Today, wives of Japanese priests are battling to be given a definite status, for their essential work for the temple to be recognized. They are also trying to receive some training.

When Zen came to the West, its rigorous training in general appealed more to men than to women. But slowly women appeared in teaching positions. Many female priests came to be ordained, and they also married and had children. This phenomenon in turn seems to have had an influence on how they teach and on how often they have deep concerns about the practice being relevant to one's daily life.

Sometimes, after having trained in Zen very rigorously and traditionally for many years, Western women realize that there might be another way of doing things and start to teach in a different format. Toni Packer is an interesting example. She became the Dharma heir of Kapleau Roshi and the director of his centre after he started to retire. She was supposed to do everything as it had been done before. Soon she realized she could not, and she began to have different ideas.

Finally, she had to break away and create a new centre. At the beginning it was very much along Zen lines with black clothes, kyosaku (stick), and many bells and bows. Soon each of these things disappeared, being seen as non-essential, too imposing and disciplining. Now only the sittings seem to remain and even then only if you want to do them. Although Toni Packer is still grounded in her Zen training she is creating a new path for her students.

She herself will say she is not Buddhist or Zen, and that she does not want any religious label. It raises the questions: When does Zen finish and something else start? Is Zen in the traditional forms and rituals, or is it in the practice only? Is a certain Buddhist environment a prerequisite? Is it still Zen if you keep the Zen practice but add it to a different religious context like Christianity or Judaism? All these questions are being pondered and worked on by many Zen practitioners in the West at the moment.

Charlotte Joko Beck, for example, trained at Los Angeles Zen Center under Taizan Maezumi Roshi, from whom she received transmission. However, she broke away from that sangha and created the Ordinary Mind Zen School which is independent. In her teaching she incorporates anything that might be useful, be it awareness/noting practice or references to Christianity, Sufism or psychology. She has also eliminated robes and titles. She does not put so much emphasis on breakthrough/kensho but more on a daily continuous practice that will help one to keep open or 'porous', as she describes it.

ZEN AND SOCIAL ACTION

Another development of Zen in the modern world is that Zen practitioners are becoming increasingly involved and concerned with social problems and issues. People are taking to heart the vows of the Bodhisattva to care for others with compassion and save all beings.

Aitken Roshi, for example, was one of the founders of the Buddhist Peace Fellowship which was created in 1978 to promote world peace. There is also the Zen Hospice Project in San Francisco which has two residential centres to care for dying people and a training programme for Zen students and other interested people to learn how to care for dying patients.

The Maitri AIDS Hospice in California was created by Issan Dorsey Roshi, a disciple of Shunryu Suzuki, who himself died of AIDS. This is a residential centre that provides housing, meals and volunteer support for people living with AIDS. There is a small meditation room and Buddhist teachers visit regularly to give talks about living and dying.

Another interesting project, The Greyston Mandala in Yonkers, New York, was founded in 1982 by the late Jishu Holmes and Testugen Glassman Roshi. It was developed as a group of companies dedicated to improving the lives of inner-city people. The Greyston Family Inn, for example, provides permanent housing and services for homeless people. A bakery was also created to give work to the homeless.

Many different sanghas are finding creative ways to help people in difficulties. Master Sheng Yen's centre, the Chan Meditation Center in New York, has established a volunteer programme, Compassion for the Dying, which endeavours to help ease the fear and anxiety of the dying and their families by providing visits, Buddhist services or meditations contributing towards a peaceful atmosphere and an acceptance of death. Other Zen practitioners are trying to help people in jail by organizing meditation classes and becoming Buddhist chaplains.

PEACE EVERY STEP

Social action is happening not only in the West but also in the East. In Korea, for example, many monks and nuns are active

through compassionate telephone lines, being Buddhist chaplains, taking care of orphans and old people, funding or giving education to children in need, managing adult education classes and leisure activities. Some Zen monastics and laypeople were also active politically when the regime was repressive.

The foremost proponent of *Engaged Buddhism* is Thich Nhat Hanh, a Vietnamese monk from the Thien (Zen) School of Vietnam. Over its long history Vietnam received both the influences of the Theravada and Chinese schools of Buddhism. Although the Zen (Thien) schools were prominent there has always been a strong spirit of tolerance among the various Buddhist Vietnamese traditions. Thich Nhat Hanh comes from such an ecumenical background. He teaches the short poems used in his Zen tradition but also the mindfulness of breathing from the Theravada sutras.

He was born in 1926. He created the School of Youth for Social Service and the Tiep Hien Order (Order of Interbeing) in 1964 to promote peace and provide relief to people in difficulties, especially suffering from the consequences of the Vietnam War. They helped by rebuilding bombed villages, developing farmers' cooperatives and starting clinics. Because he taught non-violence and not-taking sides in the Vietnamese conflict he was viewed with suspicion by both North and South and derided as a 'neutralist'. When he went to America and Europe to speak up for peace, he was declared 'persona non grata' in Vietnam and had to go into exile. This is because he organized a Buddhist Peace delegation during the peace negotiations in Paris. After the Peace Accords in 1973 he was refused entry to Vietnam and had to stay in France as an exile. He continued to devote his time to help Vietnamese refugees in France by establishing rural communities and abroad by helping Boat People stranded in various Asian countries such as Singapore. He strongly believes that in order to be socially effective we have to develop a quiet and clear mind. War cannot be cured by more war and hatred. For this reason he advocates mindfulness of breathing as a simple meditation that one can do anytime, anywhere in order to develop awareness and open our heart to the suffering of the world.

THE FUTURE OF ZEN

In the past Zen Buddhism arose in China as a result of Indian Buddhism adapting to a Chinese cultural and social context. Over the centuries many eminent teachers appeared who further transformed Zen through their creative spiritual under-standing and different personalities. Zen went on to become further acculturated in Korea, Japan and Vietnam. Now Zen is facing the modern world, be it in the East or in the West, and this will certainly lead to more transformations. It will stay alive and creative as long as it is meaningful and responds to the spiritual needs of people today. Some will find a refuge in the traditional Zen forms and monastic rituals as they give certain-ty, help, awareness and a way to express oneself artistically. Others will be more radical and feel the need to adapt Zen to their own environment and culture. Others might go through Zen and leave it behind.

As Zen is a process and an experience and not a belief, only time will tell in which weird and wonderful ways it will be taken, transformed and adapted. However, we can test its vari-ous manifestations through its two fundamental principles: wisdom and compassion.

ZEN CENTRES

There are many different Zen centres all over the world. Some are well-established monasteries where a traditional Zen lifestyle is lived and practised. Some operate only when Zen retreats are conducted. Some do not have a building as such but meet regularly in various public or private places. Many traditions established or created in the West have a major headquarters with many other groups associated with them around the country or around the world. Unless the organization has a building and a long-established place, the associated groups and centres' addresses change regularly. What follows is a partial listing, in alphabetical order by country.

AUSTRALIA AND NEW ZEALAND

Dae Kwang Sa: Queensland Zen Centre, 87 Pembroke Road, Coorparoo, Brisbane, Qld 4151. Telephone: 07 3793314.

This group is connected to the Kwan Um School founded by Korean Zen Master Seung Sahn. They organize regular sitting groups, weekends and week retreats.

Everyday Zen Group, PO Box 1626, Milton, Qld 4064. Telephone: 07 38701274.

This group is connected with the Ordinary Mind Zen School
founded by Joko Beck in the USA.

Kuan Yin Zen Centre, 183 Ballina Road, Lismore Heights, NSW 2480.

This group, led by Subhana Barzaghi, organizes regular sitting groups.

Mountain Moon Sangha, 4 Geelong Street, East Brisbane, Qld 4169. Telephone: 07 38958080.

This centre was created by Roselyn Stone who has another similar centre in Canada. She was authorized to teach by Yamada Roshi, late director of the Sanbo Kyodan School in Japan. This centre organizes regular sitting groups, weekends and week retreats.

The Open Way, PO Box 993, Byron Way, NSW 2481. Telephone: 066 854143.

This group is visited regularly by Hogen Yamahata, a Soto priest from Japan. They organize regular sitting groups, weekends and week retreats.

Sydney Zen Centre, 251 Young Street, Annandale, NSW 2038. Telephone: 02 96602993.

This centre is affiliated with the Diamond Sangha founded by Robert Aitken Roshi in Hawaii. They organize sitting groups, weekends and week retreats. They have a retreat centre near Saint Albans and associated groups in Melbourne and Canberra. They are also connected to the Kuan Yin Zen Centre and the Zen Group of Western Australia.

Zen Group of Western Australia, 29 Claremont Crescent, Claremont WA 6010. Telephone: 09 3856026.

They organize sitting groups, weekend and week retreats.

Zen Society of New Zealand, PO Box 18–175, Glen Innes, Auckland 6, New Zealand. Telephone: 09 6290562.

This group organizes Zen retreats regularly. They have connections with the Rochester Zen Center and the Zen Mountain Monastery in the USA.

CANADA

Dojo Zen de Montreal, 982 Gilford East, Montreal, Quebec H2J 1P4. Telephone: 514 5231534.

This centre is affiliated with Association Zen Internationale. It offers daily sittings.

White Wind Zen Community Zen Centre of Ottawa, 240 Daly Avenue, Ottawa, ON K1N 6G2. Telephone: 613 5621568.

This centre, directed by Zen Master Anzan Hoshin, offers residential training. The emphasis is on meditation and monastic life. There are daily sitting, various retreats and introductory workshops.

Zen Buddhist Temple, 86 Vaughan Road, Toronto ON M6C 2M1. Telephone: 416 6580137.

This temple was founded by a Korean monk, Venerable Samu Sunim. It is part of the Buddhist Society for Compassionate Wisdom. There is a programme of sitting, classes and retreats. It is affiliated with the *Zen Buddhist Temple* (312 5288685) in Chicago.

Zen Centre of Vancouver, 4269 Brant Street, Vancouver BC V5N 5B5. Telephone: 604 8790229.

This is a Rinzai centre which offers regular sitting, instructions and dharma talks. Retreats are held on Galiano Island.

FRANCE

Centre de la Falaise Verte, La Riaille, 07800 Saint Laurent de Pape. Telephone: 04 75851039.

This is a rural Rinzai centre founded by Georges Frey (Taikan Jyoji). There are scheduled retreats and also training in tea ceremony, archery and calligraphy.

Centre Parisien de Bouddhisme Zen – Kwan Um, 35 Rue de Lyon, 75012 Paris. Telephone: 01 44870770.

The two teachers, Jacob Perl and his wife Grazina, are Polish disciples of Korean Master Seung Sahn. They offer regular meditation, bowing and chanting sessions in the Kwan Um Zen School style. Weekend retreats are organized throughout the year.

Dana, 22 Avenue Pasteur, 93100 Montreuil. Telephone: 01 49889165.

This is a non-residential centre in a suburb of Paris directed by Catherine Pages, Genno Sensei, who received transmission from Genpo Roshi. There are morning, evening weekday sittings and monthly weekend retreats. Every summer a month-long residential retreat is organized in Normandy with the teaching in English and French.

Dojo Zen de Paris, 175 Rue Tolbiac, 75013 Paris. Telephone: 01 53801919.

This is the headquarters of Association Zen Internationale which was founded by the late Master Deshimaru. This centre is not residential but organizes regular sittings and one-day retreats. There are many centres affiliated with this association all over France. *Temple Zen de la Gendronniere* (02 54440486/ 54440344) is their main rural retreat centre.

Plum Village, Main address: Meyrac, Loubes-Bernac, 47120 Duras. Telephone: 05 53947540.

This residential centre is a place of practice and training for a great number of monks, nuns and laypeople. It is spread over five small holdings. It is the headquarters of the Order of Inter-being founded by Thich Nhat Hanh. It is affiliated with the Community of Mindful Living whose groups are spread all over the world. Retreats for the public are organized at regular intervals. The teachings are given in Vietnamese, French and English and translated into many other languages. Every summer there is a special month-long retreat which welcomes everyone including families and children.

GERMANY

Haus St. Benedikt, St. Benediktstrasse 3, 97072 Wurzburg. Telephone: 0931 3050410.

This Christian centre follows the tradition Sanbo Kyodan. Its director is Benedictine Father Willigis Jager who practised Zen under Koun Yamada Roshi in Japan. He teaches both contemplation and Zen. There are numerous Zen retreats throughout the year. Many groups are affiliated with this centre all over Europe.

Haus der Stille, Schweiben 2, 83229 Sachrang 1, Chiemgau. Telephone: 08057 1050.

This Christian Zen Centre is directed by Sister Fabian who did her koan study with Father Enomiya-Lassalle and Koun Yamada Roshi. This place is dedicated to meditation practice. There are daily sittings and introductory workshops as well as longer retreats.

Zen Dojo, Weissenburger Strasse 39, 81667 Munchen. Telephone: 089 4802591.

This Rinzai Zen Centre directed by Dokko-an Kuwahara offers training in meditation and Zen calligraphy. There are regular sittings and retreats.

Zen-Gemeinschaft Jikishin-Kai EV, Adalbertstrasse 108, 80798 Munchen. Telephone: 089 2719024.

This Soto Centre is under the direction of Fumon Nakagawa Roshi. Sittings and retreats are offered throughout the year.

Zen Zentrum Berlin EV, Gottschedstrasse 4, 13357 Berlin. Telephone: 030 4654793.

This centre belongs to the Korean Zen Kwan Um School. There are daily sittings and bowings and retreats are organized monthly.

GREAT BRITAIN

The Buddhist Society, 58 Eccleston Square, London SW1V 1PH. Telephone: 0171 834 5858.

The Buddhist Society offers Zen classes throughout the year.

Community of Interbeing, National contact: Val Philpott, 12 the Mount, Thornton le Dale, Pickering, North Yorks YO18 7TF. Telephone: 01751 477246.

The Community of Interbeing is the network of people in Great Britain who practise mindfulness according to the Zen Buddhist teaching of Thich Nhat Hanh. They organize evenings and days of mindfulness, retreats and other opportunities to practise together with others.

Gaia House, West Ogwell, Newton Abbott, Devon TQ12 6EN. Telephone: 01626 333613.

This is a retreat centre which holds Zen retreats, week-long and weekend, once or twice a year.

Harrow Zazenkai, 8a Butler Avenue, Harrow, Middlesex HA1 4EH. Telephone: 0181 422 9356.

This centre is affiliated with the White Wind Zen Community in Canada. There are regular sittings and occasional introductory workshops.

International Zen Association United Kingdom, 91–93 Gloucester Road, Bishopton, Bristol, Greater Bristol, BS7 8AT. Telephone: 0117 942 4347.

This group is connected to 'Association Zen Internationale', founded by the late Japanese Zen Master Deshimaru in France. They follow the Soto tradition. They have various sitting groups throughout Great Britain and Ireland in Bournemouth, Bristol, Leeds, Manchester, London, Glasgow, Cwmbran, Dublin and Galway. They also organize Zen retreats regularly.

Kanzeon Sangha UK, c/o George Robertson, Top Cottage, Parsonage Farm West, Uffculme, Devon EX15 3DR. Telephone: 01884 841026.

This Zen Association is affiliated with the Kanzeon Sangha in the USA. Its director and founder is Genpo Merzel Roshi, one of the successors of Maezumi Roshi, an exponent of both Rinzai and Soto traditions. The Kanzeon Sangha UK organizes a programme of Zen retreats (sesshins) with Genpo Roshi or Catherine Pages, Genno Sensei, whom he has authorized to teach. There are various associated sitting groups in Bury St Edmunds, Exeter, Hedden Bridge, Halifax, Hull, Halsham, Leicester, Liverpool, Maidstone, Preston, Southampton and Truro. They also have a group in Malta.

Throssel Hole Buddhist Abbey, Carrshield, Hexham, Northumberland NE47 8AL. Telephone: 01434 345204.

This training monastery and retreat centre was founded in the seventies by the late Reverend Master Jiyu Kennett when she came back to England after studying for many years in Japan in the Soto tradition. This place is affiliated to the Order of Buddhist Contemplatives which Reverend Jiyu Kennett created in America and whose headquarters are at Shasta Abbey in America.

This abbey is set in 39 acres of fields and woodlands. The main emphasis is on Serene Reflection meditation, the precepts and practice in daily life. People are welcome to visit for retreats or to join in the life of the Zen contemplatives. Every day there are five periods of meditation. People get up at 6am and go to bed at 10pm. Everyone sleeps in the meditation room as in monasteries in Japan; men and women in different parts of the room. There are about 20 to 30 men and women monastics living the Zen life under the guidance of the abbot, Reverend Master Daishin Morgan. Various Buddhist festivals are celebrated throughout the year and Buddhist ceremonies (funerals, memorials, etc) are conducted for individuals.

The *Reading Buddhist Priory* (176 Cressingham Road, Reading, Berkshire, RG2 7LW. Telephone: 0118 986 0750) and the *Telford Buddhist Priory* (49 the Rock, Ketley, Telford TF3 5BH. Telephone: 01952 615 574) are affiliated centres. There are associated meditation groups in Aberdeen, Birmingham, Bristol, Cambridge, Cardiff, Chichester, Edinburgh, Exeter, Harrogate, Huddersfield, Hull, Lancaster, Leicester, Liverpool, London, Manchester, Milton Keynes, Newcastle, Norwich, Nottingham, Preston and Sheffield. There are also some groups in Holland and Germany.

Western Ch'an Fellowship, Secretary, Simon Child, 24 Woodgate Avenue, Bury, Lancs BL9 7RU. Telephone: 0161 7611945.

The Fellowship organizes retreats in a farm, Maenllwyd, in Wales and weekends in Bristol. It is under the direction of John Crook who was authorized to teach by Master Sheng Yen. John Crook leads traditional Ch'an retreats but also Western Zen retreats and workshops on Gestalt and Zen. Maenllwyd is situated in a beautiful location deep in the hills of Wales. There is no electricity or telephone but there is hot water. The Chan retreat described in Chapter 6 takes place at Maenllwyd.

There are many groups associated with the Western Ch'an Fellowship in Bristol, Brighton, Cardiff, Edinburgh, Manchester, Stroud, Swindon and York.

White Plum Sangha, David Scott, 21a Aigburth Drive, Liverpool L17 4JQ. Telephone: 0151 728 7829.

This sangha is connected with the Kanzeon Sangha. They organize regular sittings and Zen retreats.

HOLLAND

Maha Karuna Ch'an, c/o Mariane de Boer, Vosstraat, Nijmegen, 5611 VH. Telephone: 024 3236936.

This association, which was created by Ton Lathouwers who studied under a Chinese Zen master, consists of informal sitting groups all over Belgium and Holland. Sittings and retreats are organized regularly.

De Tiltenberg, Zilkerduinweg 375, 2114 AM Vogelenzang. Telephone: 0252 517044.

This centre, open to Christian and Buddhist equally, was influenced by the late Mimi Marechal who studied Zen in Japan for many years. It started as a lay feminist Christian ecumenical centre in 1932. There are daily sittings, weekend workshops and week-long retreats.

Il Cerchio Vuoto, Via Cavour 9, 10080 Trausello (TO). Telephone: 0125 74048.

This centre is dedicated to the practice of the Soto Zen tradition. There are daily sittings and monthly retreats.

Scaramuccia – Luogo di Pratica Buddhista della scuola Linci di Chan, Scaramuccia, 05019 Orvieto Scalo (TR). Telephone: 0763 25054.

This centre, situated in an old farmhouse, follows the Rinzai Zen tradition. There are daily sittings and regular retreats.

Shobozan Fudenji – Tempio Zen Soto Centro di studi e Meditazione Buddhista, Bargone 113, 43039 Salsomaggiore (PR). Telephone: 0524 565667.

Fudenji is the headquarters of the Associazione Italiana Zen Soto. It follows a strict Soto monastic discipline. It is directed by Fausto Guareschi, a disciple of Master Deshimaru. There are daily sittings, regular workshops, retreats and seminars. Several groups are affiliated with Fudenji all over Italy.

POLAND

Stowarzyszenie Buddhyjskie Sangha Kandzeon, ul. Husarii 32, 02–951 Warsaw. Telephone: 022 427887.

This centre is affiliated with the American Kanzeon Sangha. It is under the direction of Malgosia Braunek who was authorized to teach by Genpo Roshi. Sittings and retreats are organized regularly.

Warsaw Zen Center – Do Am Sah, ul. Malowiejska 22/24, 04–962 Warsaw-Falenica. Telephone: 022 150552.

This centre is connected with the Korean Zen Kwan Um Sangha. Various retreats are offered throughout the year. There are other affiliated groups in Poland.

Zwiazek Buddystow Zen Bodhidharma, ul. Filmova 32, 04–935 Warsaw-Falenica. Telephone: 022 124757.

This centre was created after several visits by Kapleau Roshi. Now it is part of the Rochester Zen Center's affiliated groups. Sittings and retreats are organized regularly.

SOUTH AFRICA

The Buddhist Retreat Centre, PO Box 131, Ixopo, Natal 3276. Telephone: 0336 341863.

This retreat centre situated in the beautiful hills of Natal offers some Zen retreats.

Poep Kwang Sa Darma Centre, 26 White Street, Robertson, 6705 Cape. Telephone: 02351 3515.

This is a residential centre which provides a regular programme of Zen training, meditation and silent retreats. The teachers are Rodney and Heila Downey. They are associated with the Kwan Um School (Korean Zen).

SPAIN

Jiko An – Comunidad Religiosa Zen del Camino Abierto, Cortigo el Alamillo, 18460 Yegen. Telephone: 958 343185.

This centre is under the spiritual direction of Hogen Yamahata, a Soto Zen monk who visits regularly from Japan. The director, Francis Chauvet, has lived at Jiko An since 1991. Meditation and communal work are the mainstay of life at Jiko An. There are regular sittings, weekends and week-long retreats. Yoga also plays an important part in the daily practice of this centre.

Templo Luz serena – BanshoZan Wakozenji, 46356 Casas del Rio. Telephone: 96 2301055.

This is the headquarters of the Comunidad Budista Soto Zen. This centre, under the direction of Francisco Dokusho Villalba, offers regular retreats and workshops. There are affiliated groups all over Spain.

USA

Cambridge Buddhist Association, 75 Sparks Street, Cambridge MA 02138. Telephone: 617 4918857.

This centre was founded in 1958 and its emphasis right from the start was non-sectarian. For many years, the late Maurine Stuart Roshi led meditation sessions and retreats. Now George Bowman who practised in the Rinzai tradition under Sasaki Roshi and was also a disciple of Korean Master Seung Sahn is the spiritual director. Regular sittings and retreats are offered throughout the year.

Ch'an Meditation Center – Institute of Chung-Hwa Buddhist Culture, 90–56 Corona Avenue, Elmhurst, Queens, New York NY 11373. Telephone: 718 5926593.

This is an urban meditation centre under the direction of Chinese Chan Master Sheng-yen, who shares his time between New York and Taiwan. He has received transmission in both Linchi and Tsaotung lineages. Day-long, weekend and week retreats are organized.

Community of Mindful Living, PO Box 7355, Berkeley, CA 94707. Telephone: 510 5273751.

The Community of Mindful Living is affiliated with Plum Village in France, Maple Village in Canada and Manzanita Village in Southern California. Their spiritual head is Thich Nhat Hanh, a Vietnamese Zen master. They organize retreats, publish and distribute books, tapes and a newsletter *The Mindfulness Bell*. Many groups all over America are connected with them.

Diamond Sangha/Kokoan Zendo, 2119 Kaloa Way, Honolulu HI 96822. Telephone: 808 9460666.

This lay sangha was established by Robert Aitken Roshi to help people practise meditation in daily life. There are daily sittings, classes, interviews, work, celebrations and rituals. It is in association with the *Maui Zendo* (808 6697725), the first place established by Aitken Roshi which organizes meditation in various locations. The *Palolo Zen Center* (808 7351347) was created to provide residential training in a rural setting. There is a schedule of sitting, talks and retreats. The Diamond Sangha produce a newsletter *Blind Donkey*.

Kanzeon Zen Center of Utah – Hosshinji, 1274 East South Temple, Salt Lake City, UT 84102. Telephone: 801 3288414.

This centre is the headquarters of the Kanzeon Sangha which is under the direction of Dennis Genpo Merzel Roshi who received the transmission from Taizan Maezumi Roshi. This is a residential centre with morning and evening zazen, introductory courses, week-long retreats and a three-month winter intensive Zen training. There are affiliated centres in Hawaii and Illinois.

Mount Baldy Zen Center, PO Box 429, Mount Baldy CA 91759. Telephone: 909 9856410.

This centre was founded by Rinzai Japanese Master Joshu Sasaki. It follows a strict monastic training. The centre is open all year round and provides various methods of practice each season. There are many centres affiliated with Mount Baldy Zen Centre all over America.

Providence Zen Center – Diamond Hill Zen Monastery, 99 Pond Road, Cumberland RI 02864-2726. Telephone: 401 6581464.

This centre was founded by Korean Zen Master Seung San who established the Kwan Um School of Zen in 1987. There are daily meditation, chanting and bowing practices. There are retreats throughout the year of various lengths and a special three-month retreat in winter. There are many centres and groups associated with the Kwan Um School of Zen.

Rochester Zen Center, 7 Arnold Park, Rochester NY 14607. Telephone: 716 4739180.

This centre was founded by Kapleau Roshi in 1966. He designated Bhodin Sensei as his Dharma successor in 1986. This is a beautiful urban centre which offers daily meditation, various retreats, a residential training programme and introductory workshops. They produce a quarterly journal *Zen Bow*.

San Francisco Zen Center, 300 Page Street, CA 94102. Telephone: 415 8633136.

This centre was founded by the late Japanese Zen Master Shunryu Suzuki and his disciples in the sixties. They also created a monastery *Tassajara Zen Mountain Center* (Telephone: 408 6592680) and a farming centre *Green Gulch Farm* (Telephone: 415 3833134), which have been very influential in the Zen life of America. They are also responsible for a Zen hospice and a restaurant and various other activities. In the city centre and the farm there are daily sittings, lectures, courses and retreats. Tassajara Zen Mountain Centre provides two three-month retreats, otherwise it is open to the public from May until August when it offers various workshops and retreats. It is built around a hot spring. Many centres and groups are associated with these three centres.

Shasta Abbey, 3612 Summit Drive, Mount Shasta, CA 96067. Telephone: 916 9264208.

This is the headquarters of the Order of Buddhist Contemplatives of the Soto Zen Church and Zen Mission Society. Its founder, Roshi Jiyu Kennett who died in 1996, taught Serene Reflection and laid a great emphasis on the upholding of the precepts and the practice of meditation in daily life. Retreats and Zen training are offered throughout the year.

Springwater Center, 7179, Springwater, NY 14560. Telephone: 716 6692141.

This centre was founded by Toni Packer, a dharma heir of Kapleau Roshi, who could not continue in a traditional Zen Japanese way. Her style is much looser and free. Her main concern is to help people to be deeply aware in the moment. There are retreats and meditations offered regularly.

Zen Center of Los Angeles, 923 South Normandie Avenue, Los Angeles, CA 90006-1301. Telephone: 213 3872351.

This is the mother temple for the White Plum Sangha. This centre was founded in 1967 by the late Maezumi Roshi and is directed by Wendy Eqyoku Nakao, one of his successors. The Zen Center offers daily meditation, retreats, courses seminars. The teachings combine both the Rinzai and Soto Zen traditions. Their *Zen Mountain Center* (Telephone: 909 6595272), situated in the San Jacinto Mountains in Southern California, provides winter and summer ninety-day intensives, extended Zen training, and yoga, taichi, chigong, and environmental retreats. The resident teachers are Anne Seisen Fletcher Sensei, and her husband, Tenshin Sensei, who comes to England regularly to lead retreats organized by the White Plum Sangha.

Zen Center of San Diego, 2085 Primrose Drive, Willits, CA 95490. Telephone: 707 4593771.

This centre was founded in 1983 by Charlotte Joko Beck who also created her own independent school, Ordinary Mind Zen School. Retreats and sittings are organized regularly. There are affiliated centres in California and Illinois.

Zen Community of New York, 21 Park Avenue, Yonkers, NY 10703. Telephone: 914 3769000.

The Zen Community of New York is part of the White Plum Sangha. It is directed by Tetsugen Glassman Roshi who was one of the first disciples of Maezumi Roshi to receive transmission. He developed a programme to help the people in the neighbourhood. There is the Greyston Bakery and now the Greyston Family Inn, a centre for the homeless. In 1996, the Zen Peacemaker Order was also created. There are daily sittings and private interviews, Street retreats and Bearing Witness retreats in New York and abroad.

FURTHER READING

The Blue Cliff Record, Thomas Cleary (tr), Shambhala 1977.

Chan and Zen Teaching (First Series), Lu K'uan Yu (Charles Luk), Century 1960.

Catching a Feather on a Fan, John Crook, Element 1991.

Cultivating the Empty Field: the Silent Illumination of Zen Master Hongzhi, Taigen Daniel Leighton (tr) with Yi Wu, North Point Press 1991.

Diamond Sutra and the Sutra of Huineng, AF Price and Wong Mou Lam (tr), Shambala 1969.

Guide du Zen, Eric Rommeluere, Livre de Poche 1997 (in French, a very thorough guide to Zen centres all over the world).

A History of Zen Buddhism, Heinrich Dumoulin SJ, Beacon Press 1969.

Minding Mind, Thomas Cleary (tr) Shambhala 1995.

Moon in a Dewdrop: Writings of Zen Master Dogen, Tanahashi Kazuaki (ed), Element Books 1988.

The Shambhala Dictionary of Buddhism and Zen, Shambhala 1991.

The Three Pillars of Zen, Kapleau Roshi, Anchor Books 1989.

Tracing back the Radiance, Robert E. Buswell Jr (tr), University of Hawaii Press 1991.

Zen Flesh, Zen Bones, Paul Reps, Penguin 1971.

Zen Keys: A Guide to Zen Practice, Thich Nhat Hanh, Thorsons 1995.

The Zen Koan, Isshu Miura and Ruth Fuller Sasaki, Harcourt
Brace Jovanovitch 1965.

Zen Mind, Beginners' Mind, Shunryu Suzuki, Weatherhill 1973.